Harmonium and
The Whole of Harmonium

Wallace Stevens, *Harmonium*, and *The Whole of Harmonium*

Kia Penso

Archon Books 1991

8 1 1

S 846 zpen

Library of Congress Cataloging-in-Publication Data

Penso, Kia, 1959–
Wallace Stevens, Harmonium, and the Whole of Harmonium
Kia Penso
p.   cm.
Includes bibliographical references and index.
1. Stevens, Wallace, 1879–1955—Criticism and interpretation.
2. Stevens, Wallace, 1879–1955. Harmonium.
I. Title.
PS3537.T4753Z753   1991   91-22649   811'.52—dc20
ISBN 0-208-02305-4

To

Kathleen McGregor Phillips

Mama

1913–1990

Contents

———————— Acknowledgments

Alan Stephens, Professor of English at the University of California at Santa Barbara, read this book in several stages during its production. Writing this book has been a continuation of an education in poetry that began when I took his classes as an undergraduate at UCSB's College of Creative Studies.

For their encouragement I would also like to thank Professors Logan Speirs, John Ridland, and Steven Allaback.

This book would not have been finished without all the help I received from Bob Blaisdell, who carried me through the last months of work, typing from untidy manuscript as fast as I wrote it.

The following people also helped to make this book happen: my mother and father; the College of Creative Studies, which gave me teaching opportunities; Grinnell College, where during a year as Minority Scholar-in-Residence I was given the time and resources to get the manuscript into shape.

I can't imagine the book without thinking of all that they have generously contributed.

Abbreviations

Quotations from Wallace Stevens' works are cited in the text using the following abbreviations:

CP *The Collected Poems of Wallace Stevens* (New York: Alfred A. Knopf, Inc., 1954)

L *Letters of Wallace Stevens* (New York: Alfred A. Knopf, Inc., 1966)

OP *Opus Posthumous* (New York: Alfred A. Knopf, Inc., 1957)

Palm *The Palm at the End of the Mind* (New York: Alfred A. Knopf, Inc., 1971)

SP *Souvenirs and Prophecies* (New York: Alfred A. Knopf, Inc., 1977)

Chapter One

When Wallace Stevens was arranging with Alfred Knopf for the publication of his collected poems, he wanted the title of the book to be *The Whole of Harmonium*. He somewhat reluctantly agreed to the preference expressed by some "wise people" at Knopf for *The Collected Poems*, and told Knopf that it was "a machine-made title if there ever was one" (*L*, 834). It is not difficult to understand why the "wise people" would prefer a title that would announce straightforwardly to the book's buyers just what they were paying for, and Stevens was enough of a businessman to appreciate such a reason. Stevens' own choice expressed his sense of what the book represented as a poetic undertaking. The question that remains is: why, after such a long career, did Stevens choose a title that referred not to the point at which he had arrived, but to the point at which he had begun?

There probably isn't a correct short answer to that question and if there were it wouldn't tell us much. The best way to arrive at the fullest answer is by means of an inquiry into *The Whole of Harmonium*; as we become aware of its working as poetry we may have reason to be less satisfied with statements regarding it that arise out of our own speculations or preconceptions.

Stevens gives us plenty of suggestive definitions—these statements sometimes corroborate, sometimes contradict each other. As if that were not enough, we have the curious phenomenon of critics of widely divergent persuasions launching themselves off, from the same definitive statements made by Stevens, in all different directions. The trouble begins, I think, when such statements are taken out of their original context—namely, the movement of Stevens' thought as a whole, and the weight that these statements carry relative to one another within this movement.

Instead of a definition, then, I prefer to start with the sort of occasion for observation and reflection that remained a source of poetry throughout Stevens' life. Stevens had noticed and reflected on these occasions long before he wrote anything that went into *Harmonium*.

> In the afternoon I sat in the piano room reading Keats' "Endymion" and listening to the occasional showers on the foilage outside. The fronds of a fern were dangling over my knees and I felt lazy and content. Once as I looked up I saw a big, pure drop of rain slip from leaf to leaf of a clematis vine. The thought occurred to me that it was just such quick, unexpected, commonplace, specific things that poets and other observers jot down in their note-books. It was certainly a monstrous pleasure to be able to be specific about such a thing. . . . (L, 28)

Stevens was not quite twenty when he wrote these observations in his journal. As remarkable as his plainness in stating those details of the place and moment that, it's obvious, absorbed his attention for a time, is the sureness with which he summarizes not the qualities of clematis or rain or ferns or colors, but of the way reality can present itself. The grouping of "such quick, unexpected, commonplace, specific things" is an abstraction that Stevens comes within reach of through the experience of this singular event. Even as he can accurately describe the event and the qualities of it that strike him, he reflects on the significance of this peculiar state of effortless concentration, which he recollects as a "monstrous pleasure."

Which is more important? The things for their own sakes, or the renewed apprehension, through the things, of the variety and unexpectedness and presence of reality?

In the poem, "The Cuban Doctor", reality is an Indian.

> I went to Egypt to escape
> The Indian, but the Indian struck
> Out of his cloud and from his sky,
>
> This was no worm bred in the moon,
> Wriggling far down the phantom air,
> And on a comfortable sofa dreamed.
>
> The Indian struck and disappeared.
> I knew my enemy was near—I,
> Drowsing in summer's sleepiest horn. (CP,64)

This poem is not about "the monstrous pleasure" of being able to be specific and attentive to some particular object; its interest is in the apprehension of reality as something different from what is imagined. On this occasion (and it doesn't matter whether it is a real occasion or only a possible occasion), reality has other characteristics, of menace or mischief, and it is undeterred by the narrator's attempt to evade it. The Indian is one of the multiplicity of possible forms or manifestations of reality. The Indian is a singular incarnation of a generalization.

In "The Sense of the Sleight-of-Hand Man" Stevens celebrates the same kinds of occasions in the imagination that he wrote about in his journal. It is likely that he wrote this poem between *Ideas of Order*, which was published in 1936, and *Parts of a World*, in which the poem is found, in 1942. Some time between 1936 and 1942, then, would be about the time that Stevens wrote this poem. At a modest estimate, thirty-six years intervened between the journal entry and the poem.

> One's grand flights, one's Sunday baths,
> One's tootings at the weddings of the soul
> Occur as they occur. So bluish clouds
> Occurred above the empty house and the leaves
> Of the rhododendrons rattled their gold,
> As if someone lived there. Such floods of white
> Came bursting from the clouds. So the wind
> Threw its contorted strength around the sky.
>
> Could you have said the bluejay suddenly
> Would swoop to earth? . . . (CP, 222)

These encounters with "quick, unexpected, commonplace, specific things" are minor upheavals in consciousness. They are the events that make people question the assumptions they have about their experience, and how well they know it. For a lot of people, such questions are of no particular interest, and so they don't think anything remarkable has happened. They've been momentarily distracted from some purpose or goal, even perhaps pleasantly diverted. Stevens' sensitivity to these imaginative awakenings, these small reorderings of consciousness, was mature when he was very young and persisted throughout his life. His thinking about how to go from the poet's jottings in a notebook to actual poems involved him early on in thinking critically about form.

By "form" I simply mean the fact that the poem is a something on the page. I don't mean to imply anything about what its purpose relative to a reader might be: in other words, to say that a poem has a form that we can't ignore does not at all imply that as a form its sole function is delectation or the outlining of quest-romance or anything of the kind. The content of a poem doesn't have a meaningful existence as poetry except by means of form. We can't talk very profitably about poems that don't exist, and if a poem exists it has formal characteristics that come from somewhere. In my own experience as a student and as a teacher, I myself have reacted to form, and have seen my students react to form, before reacting to anything else. A strange new poem (which could be by an old author whom I'd never read before) seemed to me to be nothing but form. The formal strangenesses of Sidney's sonnets or Dryden's long argumentative poems make it difficult for a modern reader to recognize that there was once a person thinking in there. The difficulty is not insurmountable, of course; it is one that simply reminds us—as if we weren't already reminded by various contentions that have occurred in the arts in this century—that form is potent.

Ideas in poems can become forms, and as forms they may persist for even centuries because of their power to organize and rationalize experience. Poets writing about their lives have the materials of mythmaking ready to hand, and they use them. Thus, according to M. H. Abrams, some critics have taken it as a sign of bad faith or incompetence that Wordsworth did just that in writing *The Prelude*.

> Scholars have long been aware that it is perilous to rely on the factual validity of *The Prelude*, and in consequence Wordsworth has been charged with intellectual uncertainty, artistic ineptitude, bad memory, or even bad faith. The poem has suffered because we know so much about the process of composition between 1798 and 1805. . . . A work is to be judged, however, as a finished and free-standing product; and in *The Prelude* as it emerged after six years of working and reworking, the major alterations and dislocations of the events of Wordsworth's life are imposed deliberately, in order that the design inherent in that life, which has become apparent only to his mature awareness, may stand revealed as a principle which was invisibly operative from the beginning. (Abrams, 76)

Abrams on Wordsworth is to the purpose here. In *Natural Supernaturalism* he gives an account of the history of the romantic conception of the poet as a major player on—to use a familiar expression—the stage of history.

Philosophers such as Fichte, Schelling, and Hegel, imaginative writers from Blake and Wordsworth to Shelley and the young Carlyle in England, and Hölderlin and Novalis in Germany, as well as others who, like Schiller and Coleridge, were equally metaphysicians and bards, conceived themselves as elected spokesmen for the Western tradition at a time of profound cultural crisis. They represented themselves in the traditional persona of the philosopher-seer or the poet-prophet (in England, the chief model was Milton, the great "bard" of what Shelley called "the last national struggle for civil and religious liberty"), and they set out, in various yet recognizably parallel ways, to reconstitute the grounds of hope and to announce the certainty, or at least the possibility, of a rebirth in which a renewed mankind will inhabit a renovated earth where he will find himself thoroughly at home. (Abrams, 12)

The poet is a historical actor because of the visionary moments to which his sensitivity gives him access; those moments of joy in pure being, of closeness to nature, those glimpses into its real working. Here is the poet's "man among men," to use Wordsworth's phrase.

In *The Prelude* Wordsworth made his life that poet's life, a narrative of "the poet's growth." *The Prelude* has a variety of themes and subjects, but Wordsworth's aim is to relate them all to that underlying narrative movement: they are there for their own sakes, and they are there because of what they contributed to "the poet's growth:" the poet's rationalization of his experience, the poet's finding of his vocation, his place in nature.

The poet's life is given a certain form: the form makes the life intelligible. But the form itself is, in a sense, a myth. Because of the motives for its creation—the needs that it answers—and because of its power to address those needs, romantic poetry's mythology of creation had a hold on poetry that lasted throughout the nineteenth century. As a powerful myth can do, it affected the way poetry and matters pertaining to it were talked about, and it affected the way people (not all of them poets) looked at their world.

The plot of the myth has been summarized by Abrams as "a process of mental development which, although at times suspended, remains a continuum; this process is violently broken by a crisis of apathy and despair; but the mind then recovers an integrity which, despite admitted losses, is represented as a level higher than the initial unity . . ." (Abrams, 77). The myth haunts (like a walking corpse) the stylistic conventions of contemporary scholarly prose, that Graveyard of Rhetoric. Implicit in the writing of commentators on Stevens walks that old ghost, still telling the story of the romantic poet's life.

The process of mental development might be the result of the poet's own hard work, as when Helen Vendler refers to Stevens' "patient experimentation towards his own voice," but it's apparently not only his style that develops because "We keep . . . a double attitude, seeing the major poems both as things in themselves and as steps in a long progress toward his most complete incarnation of his sense of the world" (Vendler, 1969,5).

The process might be the result of forces beyond the reach of the poet, as Harold Bloom suggests:

> In 1916, about a year after finding himself as a poet with *Sunday Morning*, Stevens tried to write a long poem in *terza rima*, *For an Old Woman in a Wig*. Though we have only an incomplete manuscript of the poem, there is enough to show that it, rather than *Sunday Morning*, prophesied the mode of his major poetry to come.
>
> The reader who knows *Notes Toward a Supreme Fiction* and *The Auroras of Autumn* will be fascinated by *For an Old Woman in a Wig*, though the poem has only a mixed intrinsic value. In it, Stevens, one of the slowest developers among the major poets, tried to write a poem he was not ready to write. He made few such mistakes again, after 1916, and his canon has astonishing completeness, a sense of ripeness unique in American poetry. . . . A patient reading of *For an Old Woman in a Wig* yields little in personal revelation but deep insight into Stevens' first finding of himself as a poet. (Bloom, 22)

Bloom's argument rests on his claim that Stevens' attempt to write "For an Old Woman in a Wig" (*Palm*, 12) was a mistake because it was "a poem he was not ready to write." Such a claim can only make sense if we believe that poetry is something that proceeds independently of the poet: that when the poet attempts a poem that doesn't work out he is tampering with his destiny and is doomed to fail. Because how, otherwise, can Stevens' ambition at this point of his life, his interest in a new verse form ("For an Old Woman in a Wig" is Stevens' only poem in *terza rima*; the later poems, such as *Notes Toward a Supreme Fiction*, use three-line stanzas without iambic pentameter and without the rhyme scheme), and his brief, tentative exploration of ideas that developed from the lines of thought he had set out in *Sunday Morning* be considered a mistake? I assume that by "the mode of his major poetry to come" Bloom means the three-line stanza form and possibly the vaguely ruminative quality of "For an Old Woman in a Wig." Stevens went back to the images, tone, and themes of this fragment's most complete sections in "To the One of Fictive Music," and in the companion pieces "On the Manner of Addressing Clouds" and "Of Heaven Considered as a Tomb." From Holly Stevens' dating of the poems, it is probable that these three were written within the same year (1921-1922), not more than six years after "For an Old Woman in a Wig." Do these poems also foretell later modes?

It is curious how the language of theology has crept into the discussion of literature, until it is nearly impossible to tell whether these writers are speaking figuratively or literally. Is a poem really an *incarnation* of the poet's sense of the world, or an *objectification*? The fragment "For an Old Woman in a Wig," Bloom says, *prophesies* "the mode of his major poetry to come." "Stevens' first finding himself as a poet" is more suggestive of poetry as a religious calling than of an activity or intellectual preoccupation pursued out of interest and commitment. The application of rhetoric in the criticism of Stevens is an issue that I intend to take up in my concluding chapter.

Just as in real life, the language of theology can sound at

times like a mortician's Pre-Need sales brochure. This is Ralph Mills Jr.'s introduction to his discussion of *The Rock* as Stevens' culminating achievement:

> Poets in old age, feeling the steady approach of death, often tend to organize their attitudes, to seek out some representative symbols in which these may be embodied and preserved against the dissolution that, they fear, awaits their own persons. In such efforts they retrace the patterns of all their previous work, hoping to mount a worthy crown upon it, a final image which will suffuse each poem with a new light—an illumination wrenched from a struggle on the very threshold of annihilation. This activity is, of course, restricted by the nature of individual cases and also by the disposition of the writer's mind toward the question of last things. (Mills, 96)

The last sentence, which is the only qualification that Mills makes to this detailed statement, reduces it to literally no more than that poets in general prepare for death in the way that he describes—except the ones who, for just about every conceivable possible reason, don't. The presence of this qualification would seem to imply that the statement is intended to be factual. But it is such a tiny cargo of fact, loaded with such a ballast of qualification and metaphor, that it sinks as soon as it is launched. (Whether it is factual when applied to Stevens is another matter, one on which Mills, by his stated qualifications, has relieved us from the necessity of thinking any further.)

Helen Vendler, in *Words Chosen Out of Desire*, admits that her (and by implication the profession's) idea of the poet's development may be a fiction and not descriptive enough, but does not question its indispensability: "The fiction we construct of a poet's 'development' must be of its nature one containing many gaps; but insofar as such a fiction underlies this book, it would tell the story of a poet who had, from young manhood, great depth of feeling, but who discovered only gradually a restricted set of formal counters adequate to feeling and knowledge" (Vendler, 1984, 5). (In this version, at any rate, the poet seems less like a prophet than a really good Freshman English student.)

But J. Hillis Miller dispenses with the idea of facts altogether, and forever. Miller writes in the introduction to *Poets of Reality*: "When God and the creation become objects of consciousness, man becomes nihilist. Nihilism is the nothingness of consciousness when consciousness becomes the foundation of everything. Man the murderer of God and the drinker of the sea of creation wanders through the infinite nothingness of his own ego" (Miller, 1965,3). According to this account, Stevens is one of the poets in whom "nihilism has been exposed, experienced in its implications, and . . . transcended" (Miller,1965, 5). In the chapter he devotes to Stevens in *Poets of Reality*, Miller concedes that while "it is impossible to find a single one-dimensional theory of poetry and life in Stevens" (Miller, 1965, 259)—true as that may be—it only turns out to be so because "his poetry defines a realm in which everything 'is not what it is' (*OP*, 178)", and *this* is because "after the disappearance of the gods the poet finds himself in a place where opposites are simultaneously true" (Miller, 1965, 260). If Stevens had become aware that he was "in a place where opposites are simultaneously true," he wouldn't have had a problem. The idea of having a problem, a doubt, a question in such a place would be unnecessary, if it weren't already inconceivable. Actually, we have arrived "in a place where opposites are simultaneously true" by means of Miller's "theory" about the death of God. If you object that you don't believe the theory about the death of God, Miller can always reply that "now that God is dead, of course, you may well object but we live 'in a place where opposites are simultaneously true.' " In other words, anyone who criticizes Miller's theory, period, can't be saying anything meaningful. Nor, for that matter, can anyone meaningfully agree with this theory. That includes Miller. This is as perfect an example as anyone could want of what Karl R. Popper has called a "reinforced dogmatism".[1] No criticism, no discussion or further investigation is possible when someone uses this strategy.[2] And, in fact, Miller and the demon dialecticians of deconstruction have not progressed any further, except in a proliferation of neologisms, and even more elaborate imaginary detail, and in giving us the prospect of a succession of similar exercises, stretching on to dreary infinity:

> Beginning with the word *cure* in "The Rock," the interpreter is led further and further into a labyrinth of branchng linguistic connections going back through Whitman and Emerson to Milton, to the Bible, to Aristotle, and behind him into the forking pathways of our Indo-European family of languages. Stevens' poem is an abyss and the filling of the abyss, a chasm and the filling of the chasm. Its textual richness opens abyss beneath abyss, beneath each deep a deeper deep, as the reader interrogates its elements and lets each question generate an answer that is another question in its turn. Each question opens another distance, a perspective begun at A that begins again at B, without ever reaching any closer to the constantly receding horizon. Such a poem is incapable of being encompassed in a single logical formulation. It calls forth potentially endless commentaries. . . . (Miller, 1985, 422)

Miller's theory is an especially unfortunate instance of what happens when critics get themselves up as prophets and soothsayers. Stevens' life as a poet belongs to a whole History whose events are not of the same order as Braddock's defeat, the installation of the first telephone, or even Wallace Stevens' birthday. So Roy Harvey Pearce ties Stevens' development to the course of this special History: "In Stevens' attempts to evoke the Supreme Fiction, with the desire for transcendence supplanted by the more appropriate desire for containment, the continuity of American poetry reaches its apogee" (Pearce, 1961, 329). It is the special task of the critic to use his or her skill and sensitivity to illuminate the dim outlines of this History. Against the background of this History the poet conducts his quest: he struggles, he pauses to catch his breath : "*Parts of a World* . . . is in Stevens' work a kind of resting-place and occasion for self-assessment. . . ."(Pearce, 1965, 121) He struggles more, and in the end, of course, he always transcends: "His later work in the main records the quest of one whose reality principle was so capacious that, through the labors of the mind, it could be made to yield the very means by which it might be transcended, then enlarged—its fullest capacity at long last revealed" (Pearce, 1965,121).

Now if it were true that there did exist some kind of external force or process such as the progress of History that created and directed poets we would still have to know that force in sufficient detail and with sufficient confidence (which we don't) to be able to say with any kind of certainty how it was working on Stevens, and we would also have to know the relation of that process or force to facts that appeared to contradict it or to be irrelevant to it (which we don't). We could call this force's principles of operation The Universal Laws of Literature. Then we might have to admit that these laws were more important than the actual material checkable domain of facts in which we read the poems. But we don't have that kind of ultimate knowledge; we do have the poems, a limited amount of other writing by the poet himself, and a mass of biographical and historical fact. (I might add that sweeping deterministic mechanisms of history have been steadily falling one by one into disrepute—in the sciences, for example, where they have had to yield in the face of evidence of all kinds of contingent historical facts: new, unpredictable information, disclosure of biases on the part of their proponents.) It does not hurt to concede the conjectural nature of all the theories and expectations proposed by the critics I have been discussing. These theories are just a kind of poetry, but that may not be so terrible.

So, for instance, when Harold Bloom criticizes Stevens' explanation of "Banal Sojourn"(CP, 62), he is proposing an explanation that competes with the one Stevens has offered. Bloom's explanation ought to comprehend both the poem and Stevens' explanation.

> Stevens, with only rare exceptions, did not comment very usefully upon his own poems. This is not one of the exceptions. Of it, he remarked: "*Banal Sojourn* is a poem of (exhaustion in August!) [Stevens' parenthesis]. The mildew of any late season, of any

experience that has grown monotonous as, for instance, the experience of life" (*L*, 464). Repeated readings of *Banal Sojourn* may not convince that the malady is monotony or all of life having become a belatedness. The malady appears to be again that "no spring can follow past meridian," or that the poet feels acutely the universal nostalgia that he is now a touch old to be what clearly he never was, a "princox," a roaring boy or saucy fellow. Instead he is rather august, green and bloated like the season, "sleepy in mildew," not in "the immense dew of Florida," and damning with considerable gusto his non-Marvellian retirement into that green shade. What the poem shows, more uneasily even than the Pharynx poem will show, is Stevens' anxiety that the poetic voice in him may fail, an anxiety rendered more acute by an imaginative maturity so long delayed. (Bloom, 52)

It is certainly true that in his explanation of the poem Stevens is not trying to sound definitive or final; he is somewhat fragmentary and tentative, but nevertheless he manages to make many distinctions: he specifies a late season as an example of "any experience that has grown monotonous," of which life might be one example. Moreover, Stevens refers to "the mildew," a metaphorical term for something that accompanies or grows *on* the late season. Stevens' explanation has more information in it because it is more specific than "the malady is monotony," to say nothing of "all of life having become a belatedness." Bloom does not appear to take account of the exactness of Stevens' language in the explanation. Bloom does not say, either, how he comes to read the lines "Summer is like a fat beast, sleepy in mildew, / Our old bane, green and bloated, serene, who cries, / 'That bliss of stars, that princox of evening heaven!' " as being about Stevens himself feeling fat and old. And green. Stevens' explanation, though, is consistent with ideas and interests that he had, that he wrote about, for which evidence can be found in his letters and in the poems themselves. We have already seen how acutely aware Stevens was of qualities of reality. "The mildew of any late season" describes a quality or rather a few qualities; different ones from "quick, unexpected, commonplace, specific," but abstracting from experience in a similar way. There is no evidence in the letters or elsewhere to suggest that Stevens suffered from the kind of anxiety that Bloom ascribes to him. In order to be satisfied with Bloom's theory of anxiety, we have to disregard as unimportant much of what Stevens says: the distinctions he makes, the boundaries of his discussion, and the literal sense of the words of the poem. We end up with less than if we just read without interpreting in terms of the theory.

Even supposing we don't insist on stronger evidence than Bloom provides us with, but accept this representation of Stevens' subject and motives, we have an image of an immature, anxious Stevens, worried about his poetical prowess, feeling old and stale. How is Stevens' anxiety different from the sort of worrying about the ability to write that even a bad novelist or a dissertation writer might indulge in? Does this explanation of Stevens' motives tell us anything about the effect on us of a poem like "Banal Sojourn?" Would a thoughtful person find this commonplace anxiety more interesting than the startlingly peculiar observations of nature that are made in the poem's opening lines?

> Two wooden tubs of blue hydrangeas stand at the foot of the
>   stone steps.
> The sky is a blue gum streaked with rose. The trees are
>   black.
> The grackles crack their throats of bone in the smooth air.
> Moisture and heat have swollen the garden into a slum of
>   bloom. . . . (CP, 62)

If we are going to reinterpret and reinvent poets, the least we can do is make them as interesting as they are when they speak for themselves.[3] Ultimately it seems that the poems are not so important, since there is so much that has to be disregarded, and the poet, too, is a diminished figure. It can't help but diminish him when he is only allowed to have unconscious intentions or to be at the mercy of the forces of Literary History while the critic, enjoying the privileges of consciousness and intention, diagnoses him.

The Whole of Harmonium may well tell a story. But does it tell the old romantic story? Why should we assume that the plot of a poet's imaginary life, the life of his creations, always takes that form? The question is important because early on Stevens began to take issue with the rhetoric and postures of romanticism. Stevens' own story of "the poet's growth" bore a relation to his real life that is analogous to the relation that *The Prelude* had to Wordsworth's. But in Stevens' narrative the figure of the poet is Crispin, whose pretensions to the status of the poet as that status is defined by romanticism are just naive. Until his voyage and subsequent adventures Crispin has never reflected on poetry or on his own experience, except as his inherited concept of poetry has permitted. The production of "his couplet yearly to the spring / As dissertation of profound delight" (CP, 31) is an academic exercise. This poet's ideas about his art—about how and why he does what he does—were themselves poetic conventions. They didn't necessarily start out as poetic conventions, but that is how they have ended up.

Stevens deliberately sets up obstacles to our proceeding with our conventional assumptions and expectations, and this is all the more reason why we should be somewhat careful in how we frame our notions about his work. It is difficult to anticipate, from having read one poem by Stevens, what the next will be like. If you approach the poems with the same sort of expectations of continuity and consistency of tone and of the relation of speaker to subject that you find in, say, Sidney's sonnets, you become frustrated. This difficulty is (among other things) what Stevens means when he says in "Man Carrying Thing" that "The poem must resist the intelligence / Almost successfully" (CP, 350).

The reader of Stevens is likely, at first, to experience the poems' resistance as a lack of something: of information, of a single explanation, of a plot (such as ". . . steps in a long progress towards his most complete incarnation of his sense of the world . . ." [Vendler, 1969, 5]). One of the first, disorienting strangenesses that the reader encounters with this poetry is the lack of any discernible order or sequence from one poem to the next. Who has not at one time or another wished that the *Collected Poems* were all dated? Then one could at least grasp one poem by its relation in time to all the others. A. Walton Litz' *Introspective Voyager* (1972) is a chronological study, and a very useful one, of the development of Stevens' style. It contains information not provided in the *Collected Poems*. Dates of writing, for example, allow some poems to be grouped as a phase in Stevens' thinking. *The Palm at the End of the Mind* (Stevens, [1971], 1984), a collection of the poems edited by Holly Stevens, dates the poems in the table of contents. But if, for example, all the poems in a group were written in the same period, it becomes significant that Stevens scattered them through *Harmonium* instead of keeping them together. Why aren't poems about the same subject, perhaps even written at the same time, grouped together? Why don't solutions come after problems? The poems seem arranged more like flowers in a vase than with any intent to direct or completely befuddle the reader's expectations. Stevens did not provide this kind of information because he just didn't think it was that important. An understanding of his work did not, to his mind, require that the reader define it in terms of categories such as these. We could go even further and say that Stevens' refusal to categorize his work was a definite affirmation about the experience of poetry.

Consequently, any attempt to group or classify the poems has to be tentative and hedged about with qualifications. (Having said so much, I don't mean to imply that there can never be any justification for making groupings and categories; I only mean that when we make them, we should expect to have to modify them or discard them, or find them the least interesting thing that can be proposed about the poems, or find that other groupings just as interesting can be made.) What turns up as a central subject or theme in one poem may be nothing but an inflection in another poem. The possibility of differences in tone, in manner of addressing a subject, is itself the subject of many poems, while Stevens' awareness of the possibility shapes others, which are about something else. Stevens' practice raises doubts about the idea that there is a preset, appropriate tone for each subject or occasion. There is quite a difference between "quick unexpected commonplace, specific things that poets and other observers jot down in their notebooks," and "One's grand flights, one's Sunday baths, / One's tootings at the weddings of the soul" (*CP*, 222). A single poem, such as "The Sense of the Sleight-of-Hand Man," may treat a few topics that appear in other poems, but treat them in different ways, may make other, unexpected connections.

> . . . . It is a wheel, the rays
> Around the sun. The wheel survives the myths.
> The fire eye in the clouds survives the gods. (*CP*, 222)

These lines echo lines from the fourth stanza of *Sunday Morning*, but there the thought grows out of an argument about immortality.

> There is not any haunt of prophecy,
> Nor any old chimera of the grave,
> Neither the golden underground, nor isle
> Melodious, where spirits gat them home,
> Nor visionary south, nor cloudy palm
> Remote on heaven's hill, that has endured
> As April's green endures. . . . (*CP*, 68)

"The life / That is fluent in even the wintriest bronze" is reminiscent of "The Snow Man" (*CP*, 9) but in "The Sense of the Sleight-of-Hand Man," it is tolerable to think of "a dove with an eye of grenadine . . . / And pines that are cornets . . . / And a little island full of geese and stars" (*CP*, 222). The theme of acceptance of the imagination's creations connects this poem to other poems, each of which has an individual character. So that when you select a handful of poems on the same subject, the differences between the poems assert themselves against any single general statement of the way Stevens thought about that subject.

Moreover, the most careful reading, accompanied by relevant biographical information specific to individual poems, does not prepare you in any direct way for how Stevens will have turned experience into poems the next time around. In "Bits of Remembered Time," a short memoir, Holly Stevens recollects two places that feature in poems.

> Not far from where we lived on Westerly Avenue, from 1932 on, there was a rather muddy stream familiarly known as the Hog River. Its source was north of us, but not far away, and the upper reaches were marshes filled with cattails, reeds, and grassy hummocks; it was a fine place to walk and explore. Just beyond the bridge which spanned the Hog on Albany Avenue was a vast stretch of barren land that people used as a dump. It was full of tin cans, old bottles, rags, crates, and miscellaneous junk. It was a mess and an eyesore, but it glittered here and there on days when the sun shone.
>
> On this lot a man, seemingly coming from nowhere, built his home. A glorious shack, made of all the appropriate junk that could be found, with even a chimney: only when we noticed smoke coming out did we realize someone was living there. Since my father walked to work, and used either Albany Avenue or Asylum Avenue, he passed the lot frequently. I remember Dad saying that the occupant was a White Russian. We spent hours imagining things about him, and making up stories. (Holly Stevens, 651)

These two recollections are a gift. They give the poems an extra charge. It is satisfying to discover that Stevens had a real river in mind when he wrote "Frogs Eat Butterflies. Snakes Eat Frogs. Hogs Eat Snakes. Men Eat Hogs," and that he could have had the Hog River in mind when he describes the rivers in the poem as "nosing like swine,/ Tugging at banks, until they seemed / Bland belly-sounds in somnolent troughs . . ." (CP, 78), just as it is wonderful to know that there was a real dump with a real man on it. The real man on the dump, moreover, lives a life that looks like the life of "The Man on the Dump" (*CP*, 201), and his making a home of "all the appropriate junk that could be found" would have impressed Stevens as an instance of the idea "his soil is man's intelligence" (*CP*, 36) working success-fully. There is no uniform way to predict how such objective phenomena get turned into poems. "The Man on the Dump" is not about this man or about this dump—it's about trying to cope with the junk of poetry, and by extension the junk of civilized culture in general. Stevens uses the man on the dump, whose life is an analogy to Stevens' vision of the poet surrounded with discarded images and devices of stale, uninteresting poetry. The real man on the dump makes something really new out of all his old junk—as Stevens does with his own poetic junk. If the poem can be said to deal at all with the idea "his soil is man's intelligence," it is only as an implied afterthought to the primary concern, which is this question of what to do with poetic junk. The hog-like rivers in "Frogs Eat Butterflies . . ." are more like incidental characters or presences; they aren't central like the figure of the man on the dump, and so their relation to the prevailing concept of the poem, and to the actual Hog River, would have to be defined differently. If on reading Holly Stevens' memoir we experience satisfaction and quickened interest in the poems, it has to do with the discovery that Stevens arrived at his curious and apparently fantastic inventions by his awareness of the suggestiveness of the same objective reality that we might have experienced, that Holly Stevens herself experienced.

The account I have made of some of the difficulties in Stevens' poems is not just to show what writers on Stevens are up against. The difficulties are casual, negative indications of Ste-vens' attitude to his poetry and his idea of what poetry should be able to do. "The poem must resist the intelligence / Almost successfully" (*CP*, 350). In a series of letters to Ronald Lane Latimer, Stevens took some pains to explain himself.

In THE COMEDIAN AS THE LETTER C, Crispin was regarded
as a "profitless philosopher." Life, for him, was not a straight
course: it was picking his way in a haphazard manner through a
mass of irrelevancies. Under such circumstances, life would mean
nothing to him, however pleasant it might be. In THE IDEA OF
ORDER AT KEY WEST life has ceased to be a matter of chance.
It may be that every man introduces his own order into the life
about him and that the idea of order in general is simply what
Bishop Berkeley might have called a fortuitous concourse of personal orders. But still there is order. This is the sort of development
you are looking for. But then, I never thought that it was a fixed
philosophic proposition that life was a mass of irrelevancies any
more than I now think that it is a fixed philosophic proposition
that every man introduces his own order as part of a general order.
These are tentative ideas for the purposes of poetry. . . . (L, 293)

The Comedian as the Letter C (CP, 27) is an obvious
example of a poem by Stevens that demonstrates the use of ideas
in poetry. Crispin becomes dissatisfied with one idea, and tries
out a series of others. Each experience Crispin has is a test of an
idea—or suggests unexpected new ideas which themselves lead
him to new experiences and more ideas. Looked at this way,
Crispin's ending up at the same place where he started is not a
failure, since to arrive at this point he has awakened himself and
investigated a whole range of thought about experience that he
might have taken for granted or ignored. Throughout his voyag-
ing, Crispin does not let any single idea or program arrest his
process of questioning and investigation, even when he would
like it to.

By the way, Mr. Baker explained the title to THE COMEDIAN
by saying that the letter C was a cipher for Crispin. When I wrote
that poem, subject was not quite what it is today, and I suppose
that I ought to confess that by the letter C I meant the sound of
the letter C; what was in my mind was the play on that sound
throughout the poem. While the sound of that letter has more or
less variety, and includes, for instance, K and S, all its shades may
be said to have a comic aspect. Consequently, the letter C is a

comedian. But if I had made that perfectly clear, susceptible readers might have read the poem with ears like elephants' listening for the play of this sound as people at a concert listen for the sounds indicating Til Eulenspiegel in Strauss' music. Moreover, I did not mean that every time the letter C occurs in the poem it should take the stage. The reader would have to determine for himself just when that particular sound was being stressed, as, for example, in such a phrase as "piebald fiscs unkeyed," where you have the thing hissing and screeching. As a rule, people very much prefer to take the solemn views of poetry.

The long and short of it is simply that I deliberately took the sort of life that millions of people live, without embellishing it except by the embellishments in which I was interested at the moment: words and sounds. I have the greatest dislike for explanations. As soon as people are sure of a poem they are just as likely as not to have no further interest in it; it loses whatever potency it had. (*L*, 294)

The intelligence which the poem must resist is the reader's habitual desire to "get" the poem. The working of the letter *C*, as Stevens explains it here, is an example of the poem's resistance. The *C* sounds occur so irregularly that we are frustrated in our desire to establish a pattern for their recurrence. If we listen with "elephants' ears" for a pattern, our attention is distracted from the rest of the poem. The *C* sounds must occur in the periphery of our attention, where they work as something experienced, not known.

By the "potency" of a poem, Stevens means the way it retains its separate integrity, as an object of experience, from what we know about it. The *C* effect in *The Comedian* might seem like a relatively trivial example, but it is an easy one to check against one's own experience. In other poems, Stevens finds a variety of ways to deter us from making biographical connections: the impersonal constructions ("the mind in the act of finding what will suffice" [*CP*, 239]), the invented personages (e.g., the Weeping Burgher [*CP*, 61]) and the variety of voices and approaches to subject matter. We may consider these strategies as a

sort of perverse secretiveness, especially if we think we are entitled
to the personal disclosures that are supposedly hidden behind the
poems. But Stevens understood that the poem had a presence, a
character of sound, thought, tone, choice of words. Stevens'
poems, at first glance, resist the attempt to get hold of the
meaning of a poem or to categorize the meaning of the poem,
except on the basis of the case it makes for itself. I repeat, at first
glance: it sooner or later becomes apparent, of course, that there
are recurring themes, moods, subjects, voices. What I am con-
cerned with here is how Stevens' presentation of the poems works
deliberately against our expectations of certain familiar forms of
organization. When we try to place the recurrences in some kind
of pattern, we find ourselves in a difficulty analogous to that of
the listeners with elephants' ears.

A poem may possess its own authority, and Stevens understood that this authority had to speak for itself, even in so slight a
poem as "Earthy Anecdote."

> Every time the bucks went clattering
> Over Oklahoma
> A firecat bristled in the way.
>
> Wherever they went,
> They went clattering,
> Until they swerved
> In a swift, circular line
> To the right,
> Because of the firecat.
>
> Or until they swerved
> In a swift, circular line
> To the left,
> Because of the firecat.
>
> The bucks clattered.
> The firecat went leaping,

To the right, to the left,
And
Bristled in the way.

Later, the firecat closed his bright eyes
And slept. (*CP*, 3)

Readers of this poem, trying to make some kind of sense of it, will turn to the possibility that the creatures in it are symbolic of something other than themselves—more general feelings, qualities in abstract—because this possibility will make the poem more familiar, give us a way to master it. We don't like to be baffled. Carl Zigrosser asked Stevens the question we would all like to have asked, and got the sort of answer that Harold Bloom might consider unhelpful. "My Dear Mr. Zigrosser: There's no symbolism in the 'Earthy Anecdote.' There's a good deal of theory about it, however; but explanations spoil things" (*L*, 204). It may have been possible to give an explanation of the poem, but the "potency" of the poem, in this instance as in many others, is connected to the fact that a poem is one kind of object and an explanation is another. An explanation can be substituted in a reader's mind for the poem itself: that's how poems get spoiled. The poem still has to persuade the reader of its reality on the basis of its objective merits—what is on the page to be experienced. It may fail or succeed in doing so. To encounter a poem as an object of experience is different from describing it in terms of a theory, or even in terms of everything we know about how poems work.

Edgar Allan Poe's *Philosophy of Composition* illustrates this point, if somewhat perversely.

I prefer commencing with the consideration of an *effect*. Keeping originality always in view—for he is false to himself who ventures to dispense with so obvious and so easily attainable a source of interest—I say to myself, in the first place, "Of the innumerable effects, or impressions, of which the heart, the intellect, or (more generally) the soul is susceptible, what one shall I, on the present occasion, select?" Having chosen a novel, first, and secondly a vivid effect, I consider whether it can best be wrought by incident or tone—whether by ordinary incidents and peculiar tone, or the converse, or by the peculiarity of both incident and tone—afterward looking about me (or rather within) for such combinations of event, or tone, as shall best aid me in the construction of the effect. (Poe, 13)

Having defined the task of poetry as the creation of effects, Poe demonstrates the operation of his method in the composition of "The Raven," and thereby removes, once and for all, any doubt anyone might have had that that poem is deader than the bust of Pallas above the chamber door. It is impossible to have any curiosity about "The Raven" after reading its author's own description of what it is. "The Raven," it turns out, has only the appearance of being about anything; the appearance of being about something is just another *effect*, which is all Poe is interested in. (Instead, you feel that Poe has constructed a curiosity, some elaborate and noisy piece of nineteenth-century machinery, that vibrates and emits great clouds of smelly smoke, that leaves puddles of oil all over the ground, frightens the horses and makes the dogs bark. A machine, moreover, that doesn't do anything; it just rolls into town with the circus and you pay a penny or a nickel to watch, a little ashamed, a little horrified, a little fascinated, while it chugs and rattles away.)

Poe's ignorance of or lack of interest in reality, along with his boundless credulity as to the power of the most transparent mechanical effects (evinced here in his touching faith that the poem will survive this explanation), is about as far as you can get from Stevens' concept of the "potency" or "resistance" of a poem. Insofar as any poem has the capacity to evoke, persuade, reveal, transform, to make us curious or doubtful, it can be said to have those qualities. It's what makes people read something like *The Canterbury Tales* thirty times: the feeling that they have not apprehended everything that the work contains, that even knowing it as well as they must after the twenty-ninth time, they might have missed something, or failed to sufficiently appreciate something else, or got the feeling that something is not working for them the way it had always worked for them previously. The resistance of a poem to the intelligence is not, therefore, an absolute value of intelligibility. It's that difficulty and strangeness which convinces you, or even only makes you suspect, that all your previous expertise and knowledge are no preparation for this new experience. Stevens wanted his poems to put up obstacles to the self-complacency of knowledge with which the best of us (as Stevens did himself) have to contend. It's a very important point, and it's the point at which I think it is useful to start with all poets, and most certainly with Stevens.

Chapter Two

In 1915 Stevens submitted his new poem *Sunday Morning* to *Poetry* magazine. Harriet Monroe, then editor, selected four of the eight stanzas for publication, then added another. Stevens recommended that the selected stanzas be published in the order I, VIII, IV, V, VII, that order being necessary to the idea. (VII was the stanza that Monroe added after her first choice.) The poem was not printed in Stevens' original version until it came out in *Harmonium* in 1923, and that is the version everyone is accustomed to seeing now. People who enjoy reading Stevens' poems will have read *Sunday Morning* so many times that at least part of their feeling for the poem comes from their familiarity with its organization; I think we all retain something of that kind of habitual expectation, like children who like to be told the same story night after night. Litz points out that many people had some such feeling for the "real" *Sunday Morning*, i.e. the one they were accustomed to, which they believed was the original (Litz, 45). In other words, it is possible to rationalize our tastes in these matters when we don't have information. I don't want to underestimate the operation of habit on my own judgment of the poem, but nevertheless the difference between the two versions is so striking that I can't help wondering what Harriet Monroe was thinking, and at how easily Stevens went along with it. Did she think *Sunday Morning* was too unstructured? If she didn't have space for the whole thing, could she not wait until she did? Clearly, the poem did not impress her then in the way it seems to have impressed readers later.

Stevens' willingness to accommodate Miss Monroe is consistent with his modesty and his realistic, businesslike attitude to his work. Compromises were possible, and an arrangement could be made whereby the idea could still be communicated in an elegant way. It is also possible that Stevens did not know what he had achieved. *Sunday Morning* was a bigger poem than anything else he had done till then; it was something completely new, and opinion, even his own, had not solidified around it.

The arrangement to which Stevens assented communicates the idea of the poem straightforwardly enough. And that is the key to understanding what is not communicated by the argument alone, and it is what Litz alludes to when he says, "Although in its full eight-stanza structure *Sunday Morning* does possess a fine continuity of design, the poem is not a dialectical argument leading to some kind of resolution, and to read it it as disguised philosophy is to distort its delicate balance of voices and attitudes" (Litz, 45). This is a good place to remember Stevens' talking about "ideas for the purpose of poetry" (*L*, 293).

The argument of *Sunday Morning* is no doubt sufficiently familiar to my readers that I will spare them another explication of it, and simply refer them to any of the many fine ones that have been written.[1] The "truncated" version has the same sensible structure and the same "masterful blank verse" as the full version. But it lacks the amplitude, the sense of expansion into other dimensions, that make the full version a more complicated poem. In the "truncated" version, all the emphases are changed;

this affects the feeling, which is a big part of the development of the thought.

The distance travelled between stanzas I and VIII is lost when these two are juxtaposed, so that the woman in her thoughts leaves the contemporary world, goes all the way to ancient Palestine and back in two stanzas, and then thinks some more about her surroundings. It's as though she has never really left, as though these explorations don't have such a powerful hold on her imagination, or on the reader's imagination.

In the longer version her reflections are her journey, and eventually they bring her back to the place and time from which she started. The answers to her questions come in the course of her reflective journey; they aren't originally meant to be stagey, because Stevens is interested in the thought and the sensation of thought, and not particularly interested in stage machinery.

> Complacencies of the peignoir, and late
> Coffee and oranges in a sunny chair,
> And the green freedom of a cockatoo
> Upon a rug mingle to dissipate
> The holy hush of ancient sacrifice. (*CP*, 66)

It is important that Stevens isolates "The holy hush of ancient sacrifice" so that as a line it works against the sense of the preceding four lines. Stevens thus manages to introduce an idea like the "the holy hush of ancient sacrifice" in a way that doesn't also invoke robed priests, swaying censers, or other Gothic-style appurtenances. It's an instance of his mastery of "poetic" language. He deliberately uses the expression with a different intention from what one would expect: it's not a decorative element, as it might be in Rossetti's *The Blessed Damozel*. Here it introduces a new tension into the situation. "The holy hush of ancient sacrifice" immediately enters into an equivocal relationship with the woman's surroundings. The memory of "that old catastrophe" (*CP*, 67) is one of the objects in the room. Just like the oranges or the rug or the sunlight. The "holy hush" is supposed to be dissipated by those comfortable and pleasant surroundings, but what follows is just the opposite:

> She dreams a little, and she feels the dark
> Encroachment of that old catastrophe
> As a calm darkens among waterlights.

It might seem gratuitous but that's only because it is beautiful. It is also a marvelously apt image for one single, unique transition of thought. In fact, the way the woman's thoughts turn—from a few objects in the room to a whole inner world; layer upon layer of places, people, times, objects—belies the notion that "The holy hush of ancient sacrifice" is dissipated. Far from being dissipated, it is present in her mind, and from its great distance in time and space alters the way the woman feels about what is around her. What is one to do when ideas—in this instance, a memory of the Christian myth—make their influence felt even among these solid objects?

The sixth stanza, which Monroe completely left out, proposes a heaven that is bare and vast. "The trouble with the idea of heaven," says Stevens in a letter, "is that it is merely an idea of the earth" (L, 464).

> Is there no change of death in paradise?
> Does ripe fruit never fall? Or do the boughs
> Hang always heavy in that perfect sky,
> Unchanging, yet so like our perishing earth,
> With rivers like our own that seek for seas
> They never find, the same receding shores
> That never touch with inarticulate pang?

The call for this heaven sounds more pressing in the next lines:

> Why set the pear upon those river-banks
> Or spice the shore with odors of the plum?
> Alas, that they should wear our colors there,

The silken weavings of our afternoons,
And pick the strings of our insipid lutes![2]

This heaven is nothing but earth made nicer according to certain "poetic" ideas of decorum, comfort and beauty. These forms made for insipid poetry, and had an annoying way of interposing themselves between the perceiving mind and actuality. In "The Weeping Burgher" (*CP*, 61), " Depression Before Spring" (*CP*, 63), and others Stevens expresses the imaginative impoverishment and disconnectedness that result from this interposition. A sky that was freed from such stale and confining associations would also eventually be free for the creation of a fresh heaven out of newly discovered possibilities and values. (Stevens invented several new paradises; but the possibility that new forms might emerge was not only confined to paradise. Almost all the Florida poems in *Harmonium* are intimations of new principles of order, but there are many, many more poems that treat this theme.)

The idea of paradise is a big idea, even if after all it has been only the expression of "the need for some imperishable bliss." When Stevens counterposes the endurance of "April's green" with all the "haunts of prophecy" he is putting two great powers in opposition; but that opposition can also be felt in the nerves of the poem, in the way the poem itself, in its structure and language, suggests more uneasiness than the arguments do. The ambivalence is a reflection of Stevens' feeling. For all the arguments in favor of a mythless reality, myth is remembered here in simple and powerfully evocative metaphors: The "truncated" *Sunday Morning* ends with a vision of a possible future that will somehow have solved the problems of belief and mutability. In the short version, this accomodation or resignation seems to be a *fait accompli,* but in fact the boisterous devotion and heavenly fellowship of the men of the future will only be possible after they manage to accept that they live in an impersonal, inhuman universe that yet somehow nourishes and consoles them. The original just ends, because to accept the perishability of beauty means having to learn to live with inevitable loss, and without the consolation of philosophy. The thought in the original ("non-truncated") poem forms a structure that is more narrative than didactic. *Sunday Morning* takes everyday life as its subject in the way that a short story by William Carlos Williams takes everyday life, though it is about a different set of problems. It would be conceivable that an editor could take a short story by Williams (such as "The Farmers' Daughters") and cut and paste it in such a way that it would seem to be following a more defined argument towards an unambiguously uplifting conclusion. But to make a narrative fit a didactic argument is to simplify the special, more complicated kind of sense that a narrative makes, and to misrepresent or ignore the facts that make it complicated.

Thus, the short version begs the question of what these lines from the second stanza (also deleted) mean in relation to the whole poem and especially in relation to the sixth and eighth stanzas.

. . . . And shall the earth
Seem all of paradise that we shall know?
The sky will be much friendlier then than now,
A part of labor and a part of pain,
And next in glory to enduring love,
Not this dividing and indifferent blue. (CP, 68)

The apparent contradiction between the hope for a "much friendlier" sky and the austere paradise of stanzas VI and VIII ("we live in an old chaos of the sun") might seem to necessitate tidying up in the interest of making a tighter argument. The dramatic coherence of the long version seems to have been achieved at the expense of the consistency of the argument, but this is only true if the argument is narrowly conceived as a formal exercise that "uses" the techniques of poetry. The difficulty disappears if we treat the poem as an attack on a real problem: the yearning of the speaker to find himself in a more secure relationship with the universe—either "the sky will perhaps be friendlier" or "I will be reconciled and content living in the austere grandeur of an impersonal universe," desiring to believe one or the other of these possible descriptions of the relationship and yet unable to believe.

Stanza VIII, as the conclusion, only restates the problem by reintroducing the facts that the woman, and the speaker, have to be reconciled with.

> We live in an old chaos of the sun,
> Or old dependency of day and night,
> Or island solitude, unsponsored, free,
> Of that wide water, inescapable.
> Deer walk upon our mountains, and the quail
> Whistle about us their spontaneous cries;
> Sweet berries ripen in the wilderness;
> And, in the isolation of the sky,
> At evening, casual flocks of pigeons make
> Ambiguous undulations as they sink
> Downward to darkness, on extended wings. (*CP*, 70)

Even the last lines, so appreciative of beauty, do not give any solid assurance that beauty, or austerity, will ultimately be sufficient. Harriet Monroe evidently preferred a more upbeat ending. But years later, when Stevens was putting *Harmonium* together, he rejected some poems he had published, and he made his choice between the two versions. He had had a long time to think about it, and he was happier with the long version.

Milton J. Bates says that *Sunday Morning* is "the most frequently described as 'Paterian' " of Stevens' poems (Bates, 111), and cites a plausible passage from Pater's *Appreciations*.

> One characteristic of the pagan spirit the aesthetic poetry has, which is on its surface—the continual suggestion, pensive or passionate, of the shadows of life. This is contrasted with the bloom of the world, and gives new seduction to it—the sense of death and

the desire of beauty: the desire of beauty quickened by the sense of death. (Bates, 112)

What Bates neglects to mention (perhaps he doesn't consider it important) is that Pater, in the very next sentence, declares that "that complexion of sentiment is at its height in . . . Dante Gabriel Rossetti" (Pater, 227). By "aesthetic poetry" Pater here means specifically the pre-Raphaelites. The "desire of beauty quickened by the sense of death" belongs to the Victorians; though conscious of death, the Greeks did not cultivate morbidity. *Sunday Morning* is about beauty and it is also about death, so the question of the connection between Stevens' poem and a passage like this bears examination.

When we talk about writer A's influence on writer B, just what exactly do we mean? Pater's influence, for example, which helped to spread the pre-Raphaelites' influence (i.e. made it fashionable sometime after the fact), is attested to by Cyril Connolly, in *Enemies of Promise* :

> The Eton variety [of Milton-Keats-Tennysonian culture] was diluted with pre-Raphaelitism. Watts' "Sir Galahad" hung in College Chapel, Burne-Jones and William Morris had been Eton figures, and Mr. Luxmoore painted fastidious water colours of his riverside garden in which the fair Rosamund would not have disdained to take her medicine. . . .
>
> Another field for the pre-Raphaelite influence was in translating. Homer and Virgil were the pillars of an Eton education; it would be hard to derive more pleasure then or now than we obtained from reading them. But we read them with the help of two official cribs, Butcher and Lang for Homer, Mackail for Virgil. . . . Mackail, who had married Burne-Jones' daughter, gave to his Virgil an eightyish air, the *lacrimae rerum* spilled over and his Christian attitude to paganism, that it was consciously pathetic and incomplete, like an animal that wishes it could talk, infected everything which he translated with a morbid distress. Dido became a bull-throated *Mater Dolerosa* by Rossetti. His translations from the *Greek Anthology*, one of the sacred books of the inner culture, the very soil of the Eton lilies, were even more deleterious.

They exhaled pessimism and despair, an overripe perfection in which it was always the late afternoon or the last stormy sunset of the pagan world. . . .

To put it another way, a sensitive Etonian with a knowledge of Homer and Virgil through these translations and a good ear, would be unable to detect in poems like *Tithonus, Ulysses,* or the *Lotus Eaters* any note foreign to the work of Homer and Virgil. . . . The two classics had been "romanticized" for him, impregnated with the cult of strangeness, of the particular rather than the general and of the conception of beauty characteristic of the Aesthetic movement as something akin to disease and evil. (Connolly, 232)

Pater's influence was felt as one of the socializing forces of the unique world that Connolly lived in at Eton. Connolly conformed to the literary and social values of this world because he identified himself with it, and because he deeply wanted to be a perfectly assimilated member of it. His teachers were practicing aesthetes only a generation away from Pater but living in the same small world he had lived in, a world that had undergone almost no changes in the years between Pater and Connolly. Even Connolly's powerful desire to conform, and his success at conforming, did not succeed in doing away with his temperament and his awareness of his conformity. In other words, Pater's influence, as pervasive and concentrated as it was, did not reach all the way to Connolly's self-distrust.

In the first place, we know that Stevens' school experience was nothing like this. He didn't go to Eton; he didn't even live in England. Whatever his education might have been at Harvard, to maintain the posture of an aesthete (and, sorry to be the one with the bad news, aestheticism was part posture) would have required self-delusion or theatricalism that Stevens did not possess. The case for Pater's influence on Stevens is usually based on Stevens' having read Pater at Harvard, and his having spent some time with the Arensbergs and their friends. But Stevens seems not to have liked associating with this crowd:

I have read something, more or less, of all of the French poets mentioned by you [Mallarme, Verlaine, Laforgue, Valery and Baudelaire], but, if I have picked up anything from them, it has been unconsciously. It is always possible that, where a man's attitude coincides with your own attitude, or accentuates your own attitude, you get a great deal from him without any effort. This, in fact, is one of the things that makes literature possible. However, I don't remember any discussion of French poets; at the time when Walter Arensberg was doing his translation of L'APRES-MIDI D'UN FAUNE I knew that he was doing it, and that is about all. I am quite sure too that all that Pitts [Sanborn] ever said about blue was a casual remark by way of expressing his boredom. The sort of literary conversation that you suggest in your letter is the last thing in the world that I should be likely to engage in, except casually and quickly. In any case, I am not a good talker and don't particularly enjoy exchanging ideas with people in talk. At home, our house was rather a curious place, with all of us in different parts of it, reading. (L, 391)

Late in his life, Stevens makes two references to Pater. One mentions a book up in his attic, and the other, in a letter to Barbara Church, recollects "one of the more dreadful goings-on of Walter Pater" (L, 606). His lengthiest, most vigorous comment on aestheticism is a criticism of Swinburne's "art for art's sake" in his journal of March, 1899.

Art for art's sake is both indiscreet and worthless. It opposes the common run of things by simply existing alone and for its own sake, because the common run of things are all parts of a system and exist not for themselves but because they are indispensable. This argument is apparent to the reason but it does not convince the fancy—which in artistic matters is often the real thing to be dealt with. Take therefore a few specific examples, such as the sun which is certainly beautiful and mighty enough to withstand the trivial adjective artistic. But its beauty is incidental and assists in making agreeable a monotonous machine [cf. "Anatomy of Monotony" (CP, 107)]. To say that the stars were made to guide navigators etc. seems like stretching a point; but the real use of their beauty (which is not their excuse) is that it is a service, a food. Beauty is strength. But to perpetuate inspiration or thought, art that is mere art—seems to me the most arrant as it is the most inexcusable rubbish.

Art must fit with other things; it must be part of the system of the world. And if it finds a place in that system it will likewise find a ministry and a relation that are its proper adjuncts. Barrett Wendell says in his "Principles" that we cannot but admire the skill with which a thing be done whether it be worth doing or not. His opinion is probably just if he limits the pronoun "we" to mean rhetoricians and the like. What does not have a kinship, a sympathy, a relation, an inspiration and an indissolubility with our lives ought not, and under healthy conditions could not have a place in them. (*SP*, 38)

Stevens does not deny that beauty is a solace; he only refrains from saying that that is its sole function. This is an important distinction; Stevens' approach to beauty encompasses more than beauty: it encompasses facts and experiences in which neither the aesthetes nor the pre-Raphaelites had any interest. As we have already seen, *Sunday Morning* is unsure about the sufficiency of beauty, and critical of some concepts of it. In "Anatomy of Monotony" (*CP*, 107), "To the One of Fictive Music" (*CP*, 87), and "On the Manner of Addressing Clouds" (*CP*, 55) Stevens questions the idea of beauty. From early as 1899, then, and consistently through his writing we find that Stevens is at variance with aestheticism in this essential particular. Stevens' ideas about the figure of the poet, and in fact Stevens' own career, corroborate this. He didn't think there was any conflict between his poetry and his work in the insurance business. Aside from the fact that he wrote and published poetry, nothing in the external circumstances of his life would indicate he was a poet. And, of course, there were people who worked with him who did not know—at least until fairly late in Stevens' life.

In the second place, from his journals we know that aside from Pater, Stevens also thoughtfully read Palgrave, Jowett, and Paul Elmer More. He gave a great deal of attention to Paul

Elmer More. He read, and carried around with him the intellectual platitudes of his day, just as we do those of our day. None of the other people who had the same education wrote "The Emperor of Ice-Cream " (CP, 64). Pater's influence, given these considerations, can only be considered very slight, or at any rate is not of a kind that makes its presence known in the facts of Stevens' life, in his ideas about poetry, or even in his practice. Stevens does not use the pre-Raphaelites' revived paganism in *Sunday Morning*; his Jove is wilder and more archaic: "He moved among us as a muttering king / Magnificent, would move among his hinds" (CP, 68). The Christianity that Stevens evokes is also harsher and barer: that "ancient sacrifice" with its connotation of human sacrifice does not lend itself to the style of Christianity of Rossetti's *The Blessed Damozel*. The youths and maidens of *Sunday Morning* all seem quite robust and healthy; they don't show any interest in, or fear of, the little reminders that death scatters around them. The influence of Pater on Stevens is so hedged about with qualifications and reservations that it dwindles to a very paltry thing as against the very strong motives Stevens had for writing in the way he did.[3] What is much worse, the arguments themselves which are used to account for Pater's influence also obscure Stevens' own purposes. "Insofar as there is a cosmology behind the 'new Cyrenaicism' of Pater's Marius or the 'new hedonism' of Wilde's Dorian Gray, it is the same that informs the conclusion of 'Sunday Morning' " (Bates, 113). Perhaps it's his awareness of these difficulties that makes Bates confine this assertion to the similarities between the three writers. Wilde, a student of Pater's, also had his own agenda; there is no "cosmology" in *The Picture of Dorian Gray*, which is about an even more specialized social milieu than Connolly's, and in which Wilde thinly disguises the sexuality of its constituents as hedonistic, aesthetic eccentricity. Pater would not have taken such a risk, but Wilde might have found in Pater's own paganism and aestheticism—the outlet, among other things, of Pater's own repressed sexuality—another perfect cover. It was part of the fun that people should be in on the masquerade (that is, to know that it was not masquerade but actual identity), and in this Wilde seems to have overestimated his public's sense of humor. Between Pater, Wilde, and Stevens we discover three quite different motivations: Pater's "Cyrenaic hedonism" (Connolly: "The artistic fault of the Cyrenaic philosophy is a tendency to fake these golden moments, inevitable when they are regarded as the only ones worth living for; the artist becomes like the medium who has to produce a psychic experience to earn her money. . . . [cf. Pater's *Imaginary Portraits*]" (Connolly, 50). Wilde's "new hedonism"; and Stevens in *Sunday Morning,* attempting to develop belief out of immediate conditions, and finding out just how complicated immediate conditions really are.

To identify *Sunday Morning* as created under the influence of Pater is to say something that may be true (can't be proven to be untrue) but is inert. It does not bring you any closer to the way Stevens' creative intelligence actively questioned itself. The way to get a sense of that is to examine critically, not Stevens' positions on contemporary debates in aesthetics, but the statements he makes in his poems and elsewhere for what they reveal about where his deepest concerns lie. More important than what Stevens read is the way he liberated himself from it, not in order to be "original" (i.e. come up with a new angle) or "contemporary" (i.e. keep up with the age's image of itself), but in order to tell the truth of his experience.

Wordsworth, going back to Milton, found something in Milton's grand style that suited his particular purposes, which were not the same as Milton's. Wordsworth chose Milton's influence, specifically for a grandeur of style that he found equal to the grandeur of his own subject and his feelings about that subject. But what Wordsworth had to say in some of his most Miltonic passages about the relationship between nature and the human spirit, and about the sources of religious inspiration, would have seemed to Milton contemptible or blasphemous: probably both. Stevens and Wordsworth wanted to resist the other, more pervasive and dangerous kind of influence—that which identifies a certain form with a particular subject, or a style with a particular topic. Such forms and tones may be contemporary cant, or they may simply not suit the needs of a particularly original thinker who comes along. Thus, when corset salesmen in eighteenth-century England began to talk about "finnyprey," or the writers of frantic little pamphlets on issues of the day struck mock heroic poses, they were using the style and idiom of Pope in ways for which Pope need not be held responsible. So much is conceded by Wordsworth in the "Preface to the Second Edition of the *Lyrical Ballads.*"

> Without being culpably particular, I do not know how to give my Reader a more exact notion of the style in which it was my wish and intention to write, than by informing him that I have at all times endeavoured to look steadily at my subject; consequently, there is I hope in these Poems little falsehood of description, and my ideas are expressed in language fitted to their respective importance. (Wordsworth, 323)

Wordsworth is of course referring to the style of the ballads. He probably did not have to anticipate equally strong objections to the blank verse poems. But the point still holds—that the style, the language of a poem, is determined first by the poet's attention to his subject.

> Something must have been gained by this practice, as it is friendly to one property of all poetry, namely good sense: but it has necessarily cut me off from a large portion of phrases and figures of speech which from father to son have long been regarded as the common inheritance of Poets. I have also thought it expedient to restrict myself still further, have abstained from the use of many expressions, in themselves proper and beautiful, but which have foolishly been repeated by bad Poets, till such feelings of disgust are connected with them as it is scarcely possible by any art of association to overpower. (Wordsworth , 323)

The forms that ideas take, the inflections of tone of particular words, the stock images are all a battery of poetical resources that can be used to give energy and an appearance of authority to writing that has other purposes than telling, or even trying to discover, the truth of the writer's experience: writing that has as its subject the virtues of tooth powder or candidates for political office. This kind of writing is governed by the law of diminishing returns: after all, even a dog won't let you play the same trick on him three times. Wordsworth is not picking a quarrel with a tradition here, so much as he is declaring his resolution to fight the dominance of forms that are no longer capable of either awakening consciousness or facilitating its contact with reality. Before the "common inheritance of Poets" becomes disgusting, it becomes narcotic, even oppressive. These usages seem to be the very structure of reality; the only terms in which poems can be written. Wordsworth achieved his victory over that oppression and disgust by writing his poems that made it possible to displace old forms, and, most importantly, by honoring his sensitivity to language and to the unique character of his experience. Wordsworth's hope that "there is little falsehood of expression" and that the ideas are "expressed in language fitted to their respective importance" implies that he has relied on his own feeling and judgment, as opposed to the standards of common practice, to direct him in his work.

And, of course, there were and are still people who could, and can, take an intelligent pleasure in the writing of Pope. What Wordsworth is proposing in the passage quoted above (I won't say that it's true for the whole "Preface") is not dogma, not ideology, but activity. If there is any progress, it's not the whole of humanity marching confidently forward, all in the same direction, in the certainty that wherever we are going is better than here and anyone who can't or won't keep up with the march does not deserve to get there and if they do get there will probably just end up making things disagreeable for everybody. The activity Wordsworth is proposing is the play of the mind on what it thinks it knows inside and outside itself, and it is the most interesting way the mind has of getting to know itself.

The "Preface" is a real manifesto. Stevens is far more diffident about his powers than Wordsworth, and that's partly because Wordsworth just had more nerve generally. The difference may also have something to do with the times they lived in. Wordsworth in *The Prelude* could remember the historical optimism that the French Revolution kindled in himself and others: "Bliss was it in that dawn to be alive, / But to be young was very heaven!" (Wordsworth, 252) Even after he became disillusioned with revolutionary politics, the romantic poet's sense of a special historic destiny—as a poet and not as a political activist— endured. The counterpart to Wordsworth's historic sense is Stevens' "I would like to be a St. Augustine but modernity is so Chicagoan" (*L*, 32). Stevens did not try to escape or defy the time and environment in which he felt he had to write. He knew all too well that he couldn't be a poet according to Wordsworth's or Shakespeare's conception of the poet. Not from any lack of capacity, because he certainly had the resources; but because it wouldn't be appropriate, it would be false to the world he lived in.

He didn't write a manifesto; he didn't make public proclamations that declared what needed to be done and how he was going to do it. He didn't, as Wordsworth could be said to have done, substitute the authority of Nature for the authority of Tradition. Everything had to happen in the surface of the poem, in its language, in its power to engage the mind of the reader. He had to tell the truth of his experience, on his own, watchful against ready-made conceptions of that experience. Such uncertainty as he infrequently expresses—for example in this letter to Harriet Monroe—has its source in the fact that he was doing something new, he didn't have a tradition of rules and conventions that gave authority to what he did, to which he could appeal. Although he worked with the conventions of the grand style, he was doing new things with them.

> Gathering together the things for my book has been so depressing that I wonder at *Poetry*'s friendliness. All my earlier things seem like horrid cocoons from which later abortive insects have sprung. The book will amount to nothing, except that it may teach me

something. I wish that I could put everything else aside and amuse myself on a large scale for a while. One never gets anywhere in writing or thinking or observing unless one can do long stretches at a time. Often I have to let go, in the most insignificant poem, which scarcely serves to remind me of it, the most skyey of skyey sheets. And often when I have a real fury for indulgence I must stint myself. Of course, we must all do the same thing. Ariosto probably felt the same thing about the solid years he spent on Orlando. If farmers had summers ten years long what tomatoes they could grow and if sailors had universal seas what voyages they could take. Only, the reading of these outmoded and debilitated poems does make me wish rather desperately to keep on dabbling and to be as obscure as possible until I have perfected an authentic and fluent speech for myself. By that time I should be like Casanova at Waldheim with nothing to do except look out of the windows. (*L*, 231)

He needs to find an "authentic and fluent speech" for himself because no other way will do. What "authentic and fluent speech" means for Stevens is not just a new manner or pose: "To my way of thinking, there is not the slightest affectation in anything I do. I write as I do, not because that satisfies me, but because no other way satisfies me " (*L*, 287).

In the following passage from a letter to another correspondent, Stevens takes care to define the character of the paganism that emerges in *Sunday Morning*. The reason that Stevens' paganism here is different is that it comes from different sources, it has a different motivation. Stevens seems to mean to suggest that to meditations and questionings such as those in *Sunday Morning*, an answer might take the form of a new kind of paganism, one that builds itself out of a new contact of the mind with itself and its environment. Such an emergence of tentative answers is like the finding of "an authentic and fluent speech." The process of question and response, and what it creates or discovers, is what remains constantly important to Stevens.

[*Sunday Morning*] is not essentially a woman's meditation on religion and the meaning of life. It is anybody's meditation. To judge from your comment on it, you are taking the thing a little too literally. The poem is merely an expression of paganism, although, of course, I did not think that I was expressing paganism when I wrote it. (*L*, 250)

In the last statement, which sounds unsolicited, Stevens rejects outright the possibility that he wrote *Sunday Morning* out of a desire to revive paganism. The nineteenth century was, of course, great for revivals. Tennyson went back to Homer and to something that could be called "barefoot Gothic." Browning's dramatic monologues are organized around a conception of the Italian Renaissance that could be summarized as a philosophy (and was, by Santayana). Yeats wrote pre-Raphaelite poems, and long after he got out from under their influence he took up the old Celtic mythology. Some of Pound's best poems are revivals; his life work was the revival of paganism (which got somehow muddled in with his program for economic reform). Pound had a sense of mission; he wanted to change the world; he talked with politicians and allied himself with the political groups whose program most resembled his own. Of course, Pound's political and historical judgment were execrable; the people whose economic and political program most resembled his own were the fascists. But if there has been one good consequence to that catastrophe, it is that Pound has to be read with a certain care; we can't ever feel removed from the ethical questions that reverberate around his work.

All these writers' excursions into the past were made with the intention of fetching something back that they felt was lacking in their own time. Their attitude to the present (their present) can be adduced from what they took with them into the past. (Compare Pound's *Canto I* and Tennyson's "Ulysses": that tiny figure approaching from the fading margin of that untravelled world is Kipling, and Ulysses could just as easily be Queen Victoria decked out as Boadicea.)

Stevens did not have any interest in a revived or artificial paganism. Pound and the nineteenth century English poets believed that something essential to real poetry was lacking in their time and had to be borrowed from the past. Stevens found plenty of poetry in his own experience. We have already seen his appreciation of "quick, unexpected, commonplace, specific things." He was also susceptible to larger, more general impressions:

> In the early part of the day I saw some very respectable country which, as is usual, set me contemplating. I love to walk along with a slight wind playing in the trees about me and think over a thousand and one odds and ends. Last night I spent an hour in the dark transept of St. Patrick's cathedral where I go now and then in my more lonely moods. An old argument with me is that the true religious force in the world is not the church but the world itself: the mysterious callings of Nature and our responses. What incessant murmurs fill that ever-laboring, tireless church! But to-day in my walk I thought that after all there is no conflict of forces but rather a contrast. In the cathedral I felt one presence: on the highway I felt another. Two different deities presented themselves: and, though I have only cloudy visions of either, yet I now feel the distinction between them. The priest in me worshipped one God at one shrine; the poet another God at another shrine. The priest worshipped Mercy and Love; the poet, Beauty and Might. In the shadows of the church I could hear the prayers of men and women; in the shadows of trees nothing human mingled with Divinity. As I sat dreaming with the Congregation I felt how the glittering altar worked on my senses stimulating and consoling them; and as I went tramping through the fields and woods I beheld every leaf and blade of grass revealing or rather betokening the Invisible. (*L*, 58)

Between the two ends of the scale—the self-sufficiency of particulars and the invisible presence that may or may not hold a complex world in an intelligible order—there was a whole range of experiences that continually challenged his ideas about it. This challenge provoked and troubled Stevens. When we consider the resources of poetic idiom at his command, it seems strange that he should be writing to Harriet Monroe in 1922 about his not having achieved "an authentic and fluent speech for [him]self," and referring to the poems in *Harmonium* as "abortive insects" (*L*, 231). This remarkable letter reveals something of Stevens' sense of the difficulty of writing a true poem, according to his conception of what poems had to do. He had to struggle with experience, with the poem, and with his ideas about both experience and poetry. He carried out this struggle on his own; he didn't argue about it in coffee shops, or write manifestos. He didn't go on the lecture circuit putting the arguments and the issues before the public; he worked on it in the poems. He was very busy with his own experience, too busy with it to do what other people were doing.

Ploughing On Sunday

The white cock's tail
Tosses in the wind.
The turkey-cock's tail
Glitters in the sun.

Water in the fields.
The wind pours down.
The feathers flare
And bluster in the wind.

Remus, blow your horn!
I'm ploughing on Sunday,
Ploughing North America.
Blow your horn!

Tum-ti-tum,
Ti-tum-tum-tum!
The turkey-cock's tail
Spreads to the sun.

The white cock's tail
Streams to the moon.

Water in the fields.
The wind pours down. (CP, 20)

Chapter Three

I began with the suggestion that we ought to be careful in the use of *a priori* assumptions and definitions when reading Stevens. For example, taking the tone or attitude of a poem like "The Snow Man" as representing the dominant theme or problem for Stevens, or taking a simple schematic opposition, as, say, between "The Snow Man" and other poems of bareness and setting them against the Florida poems. In my discussion of *Sunday Morning* I tried to show how the dramatic movement of the poem itself implies many of the questions that persisted for Stevens throughout his career. In the tension between the explicit and implicit in *Sunday Morning* we can clearly see suspended the central issues of Stevens' poetry. *Sunday Morning* reflects on Stevens' other poems, but they in turn talk back, in a multiplicity of voices.

The current tendency is to look at the earlier poems as sort of experimental squibs that occasionally show the rough beginnings of the greatness to come, as though Stevens did not yet have the capacity for reflection on his art. *The Comedian as the Letter C* doesn't really fit into this scheme of steady progress. I intend to show in the present chapter that *The Comedian*, like *Sunday Morning*, has a lot to say about what Stevens had written so far, and about what he would subsequently write. The poem is a synthesis, in the form of a narrative, of Stevens' sense of what he had done and what he might be able to do. It should be of interest to us that Crispin's adventures end so inconclusively. Crispin is back where he began; he is not sure that he has transcended anything because the same old questions (and some new ones) still haunt him. Similarly, for Stevens, the same questions recur, and he kept on writing poems that do not show any "progress" toward a complete resolution. *The Comedian* surveys many of the statements, oppositions, and problems that one finds in Stevens' work and sets them in one possible relation to each other. *The Comedian's* subject is how the poet uses his assumptions and ideas, and how even after he has discarded them he may not be finished with them.

The Comedian as the Letter C starts with the statement "man is the intelligence of his soil" (*CP*, 27); the statement is plausible and has the respectability of ancient lineage, going back at least as far as the book of Genesis. Stevens specifies some of its implications: "As such, the Socrates / Of snails, musician of pears" (*CP*, 27). In these manifestations, the role has an incontrovertible, dignified and elegant irrelevance. Crispin may not be aware of it, but there are aspects of man[1] in the character of "sovereign ghost" (*CP*, 27) that resemble nothing so much as bureaucrats with inflated titles.

In the ordinary course of his life Crispin with "an eye of land, of simple salad-beds, / Of honest quilts" becomes intrigued at the sight of porpoises in the sea (*CP*, 27). When he sets out to sea he has no intention of challenging the idea of man's sovereignty or questioning the image of himself that sovereignty implies. He has an intuition—"What mattered was mythology of self / Blotched out beyond unblotching" (*CP*, 28)— but he hasn't

yet experienced what it might mean for his ideas and his life. He
sets out believing that the relationship between himself and the
"soil" will be maintained, only expanded in its range to include
the sea and its contents. "One eats one paté, even of salt,
quotha."

> . . . . Crispin,
> The lutanist of fleas, the knave, the thane,
> The ribboned stick, the bellowing breeches, cloak
> Of China, cap of Spain, imperative haw
> Of hum, inquisitorial botanist,
> And general lexicographer of mute
> And maidenly greenhorns, now beheld himself,
> A skinny sailor peering in the sea-glass.
> What word split up in clickering syllables
> And storming under multitudinous tones
> Was name for this short-shanks in all that brunt?
> (CP, 28)

After portraying Crispin in this torrent of words ("lutanist of
fleas" (CP, 28): Stevens frequently makes the lute the instrument
of choice of the bland romantic poet), Stevens describes what has
happened to Crispin in the simplest, plainest declarative sentence: "Crispin was washed away by magnitude."

The overwhelming vastness of the sea—only one of its
important characteristics to Stevens—also impresses the Doctor
of Geneva, in spite of his being able to maintain an appearance
of decent self-control.

> He did not quail. A man so used to plumb
> The multifarious heavens felt no awe
> Before these visible, voluble delugings,
>
> Which yet found means to set his simmering mind
> Spinning and hissing with oracular
> Notations of the wild, the ruinous waste,

> Until the steeples of his city clanked and sprang
> In an unburgherly apocalypse.
> The doctor used his handkerchief and sighed. (CP, 24)

That the sea (or ocean) is larger than your ideas about it is obvious to anyone who has been out of sight of land in a small boat. And it is hardly a new idea in fiction or poetry. We might remember here Keats' sonnet "On First Looking into Chapman's Homer," where to suggest what Chapman's Homer meant for him he sketches a mythical discovery of the Pacific Ocean (I say "mythical" because while the Pacific Ocean was undoubtedly "discovered," it was Balboa who discovered it, not Cortez).

> Then felt I like some watcher of the skies
>   When a new planet swims into his ken;
> Or like stout Cortez when with eagle eyes
>   He star'd at the Pacific—and all his men
> Look'd at each other with a wild surmise—
>   Silent, upon a peak in Darien. (Keats, 1126)

Keats' Cortez and his men are speechless because the Universe that they live in has changed. Cortez has discovered now that he does not *know* it, that there is a different scale by which human experience, and human life, can be defined. Your identity, your "mythology of self," may be no match for this experience, even an identity as well established as that of the Doctor. He suppresses (though not altogether successfully) the "unburgherly apocalypse" the ocean sets off in his mind—he is a tough old Calvinist after all—but Crispin surrenders to the new relation between himself and the world and is never the same again. Without the experience of the dissolution of almost all of himself in this impersonal and powerful vastness, Crispin's other adventures could not happen. Stevens writes again about the proper scale for defining human experience in "In the Clear Season of Grapes."

The mountains between our lands and the sea—
This conjunction of mountains and sea and our lands—
Have I stopped and thought of its point before?

The first stanza takes note, perhaps for the first time to the speaker (one of Stevens' characters) of a relationship, a "conjunction," not designed by himself.

> When I think of our lands I think of the house
> And the table that holds a platter of pears,
> Vermilion smeared over green, arranged for show.
>
> But this gross blue under rolling bronzes
> Belittles those carefully chosen daubs.
> Flashier fruits! A flip for the sun and moon,
>
> If they mean no more than that. But they do.
> And mountains and the sea do. And our lands.
> And the welter of frost and the fox cries do.
>
> Much more than that. Autumnal passages
> Are overhung by the shadows of the rocks
> And his nostrils blow out salt around each man.
> (CP, 110)

The "carefully chosen daubs" of the pears on the table, "arranged for show" provide an aesthetic experience, but here an aesthetic experience is a trivial experience. If the sun and the moon were nothing but "flashier fruits"—the same thing, just more of it—they would also be trivial. But when the speaker recognizes the "conjunction of mountains and land and sea," he also discovers himself in a relation to it that is much more essential: "his nostrils blow out salt around each man." The poem restates Stevens' criticism of "art for art's sake,"[2] but this time Stevens writes in just one of the new poetic idioms he has devised, since the writing of the journal entry.

As for Crispin,

The dead brine melted in him, like a dew
Of winter, until nothing of himself
Remained, except some starker, barer self
In a starker, barer world, in which the sun
Was not the sun because it never shone
With bland complaisance on pale parasols,
Beetled, in chapels, on the chaste bouquets. (CP, 29)

Crispin's encounter with the sea, by changing his self-definition
also changes the way he responds and acts.

The sea
Severs not only lands but also selves.
Here was no help before reality.
Crispin beheld and Crispin was made new.
The imagination, here, could not evade,
In poems of plums, the strict austerity
Of one vast, subjugating, final tone. (CP, 30)

Crispin has attained a tragic knowledge: he has learned that selves
can be severed—not only in death but in the indifferent hugeness
of the external world. When he seemed—except for a few
speculative fancies—to know everything, he was only ignorant of
his own incompleteness. Now he knows it, and his need for "a
mythology of self" is more than just a poetic idea. His incompleteness, the fact that he doesn't (and didn't before though he
thought he had) know what he is, has moved from the fringes of
poetic speculation to the center of consciousness, where he now
finds self-delusion intolerable. What passed previously with him
for knowledge of life will not do any more, while at the same
time he is liberated. His eyes have been opened. "He was a man
made vivid by the sea, / A man come out of luminous traversing"
(CP, 30).

Crispin's transformation awakens his energies, and this is a
beginning for him. Now that he has emerged from his own
dissolution, his curiosity is quickened, he is restless.

How greatly had he grown in his demesne,
This auditor of insects! He that saw
The stride of vanishing autumn in a park
By way of decorous melancholy; he
That wrote his couplet yearly to the spring,
As dissertation of profound delight,
Stopping, on voyage, in a land of snakes,
Found his vicissitudes had much enlarged
His apprehension, made him intricate
In moody rucks, and difficult and strange
In all desires, his destitution's mark. (CP, 31)

(For all of his new capacities, he may only be "as other freemen are, / Sonorous nutshells rattling inwardly" because Stevens won't allow Crispin, or other freemen, an exaggerated "romantic" sense of their own importance.)

Crispin rediscovers writing.

He perceived
That coolness for his heat came suddenly,
And only, in the fables that he scrawled
With his own quill, in its indigenous dew. . . . (CP, 31)

But writing now means something different from what it has previously. If the earlier Crispin wrote out of a false but flattering image of himself in relation to nature, he wrote in accordance with a socially recognized convention, the pose of the poet. That image was false because the language of it was no longer valid— was not drawn from the right kind of attention to, and engagement in, experience. It was flattering because it had a grandeur about it; but that grandeur was not authentic any more—it had become an empty ceremoniousness of diction. Crispin is not interested any more in writing as a social function in that sense because writing now has a more urgent and potentially enriching purpose: to maintain or extend his truer, more vivid contact with the world around him.

In a letter to Ronald Lane Latimer, Stevens defends himself against the suggestion that his style is affected. Some of the details of the exchange have to be sketched in, but it seems that Latimer made the suggestion to Stevens that his style compares with the highly mannered style of Ronald Firbank's fiction. Stevens objects because Firbank's style was motivated in a very different way from his own.

> There may be some similarity between his work and mine, but certainly there is no relation between the two things. This is extremely interesting. It raises the question why one writes as one does. To my way of thinking, there is not the slightest affectation in anything I do. I write as I do, not because that satisfies me, but because no other way satisfies me. It is curious to think that Firbank wrote in the way he wrote for the same reason. (L, 287)

But in the next letter he goes even further with this than a mere defense of his style, coming close to a definitive statement of why he does what he does.

> This leaves two questions: Whether I accept the common opinion that my verse is essentially decorative, and whether my landscapes are real or imagined. I have delayed answering your letter because I was on the point of saying that I did not agree with the opinion that my verse is decorative, when I remembered that when HAR-MONIUM was in the making there was a time when I liked the idea of images and images alone, or images and the music of verse together. I then believed in *pure poetry*, as it was called.
>
> I still have a distinct liking for that sort of thing. But we live in a different time, and life means a good deal more to us now-a-days than literature does. In the period of which I have just spoken, I thought literature meant most. Moreover, I am not so sure that I don't think exactly the same thing now, but, unquestionably, I think at the same time that life is the essential part of literature.
>
> Again, life is the normal thing to which I referred in my last letter to you. I don't at all like the words *decorative* and *formal*. Here in Hartford one gets a different reaction; here people who speak about the thing at all speak of my verse as aesthetic. But I don't like any labels, because I am not doing one thing all the

time; it may look very much like one thing, just as it seems entirely
without ideas, which, from my point of view, is ridiculously wrong.
However, for all that, it is ridiculously wrong to object to such
comments.

While, of course, my imagination is a most important factor,
nevertheless I wonder whether, if you were to suggest any particular
poem, I could not find an actual background for you. I have been
going to Florida for twenty years, and all of the Florida poems have
actual backgrounds. The real world seen by an imaginative man
may very well seem like an imaginative construction. (*L*, 288–289)

He then goes on in this letter to talk about the poem "Mr.
Burnshaw and the Statue" (*OP*, 46).

You will remember that Mr. Burnshaw applied the point of view of
the practical Communist to IDEAS OF ORDER; . . . I have tried
to reverse the process; that is to say, apply the point of view of a
poet to Communism. Even in its present condition I should be
able to trace a process of thought: analyse for you what I have
written, and by that means illustrate by a poem which might seem
largely gaseous the sort of contact that I make with normal ideas.
(*L*, 289)

Three phrases from this passage stand out: first, " the point of
view of the poet." Here Stevens implies that the critic (Marxist or
otherwise) does not exclusively enjoy the privilege of having a
point of view; poetry in its own way is as polemical as criticism.
The second and third go together. He speaks of tracing "a process
of thought" and of the "contact he makes with normal ideas."
He has put all this so carefully, has been so scrupulous to avoid
ready-made ways of talking about these things, that it is worth
seeing how it all comes together in the last paragraph of the
letter.

These remarks alone will show that my principal concern with this
poem (and, I suppose, with any poem) is not so much with the
ideas as with the poetry of the thing. I came across an amusing
incident of the opposite in an English paper the other night: [Sir
James George] Frazer, the GOLDEN BOUGH man, wrote a

poem for the purpose of calling Mussolini a dirty dog. It was a
typical poem of ideas. Frazer was not enough of a poet to make a
go of it, but if he had been: if he had been able to express the very
general condemnation of Mussolini . . . , he would have been a
typical poet of ideas. I cannot say that I do not think such a poet
should be the chief figure among poets. Unfortunately, I don't
have ideas that are permanently fixed. My conception of what a
poet should be and do changes, and I hope, continually grows. (*L*,
288)

(He seems never to have satisfactorily worked out the difficulties he mentions having with "Mr. Burnshaw and the Statue,"
and that is probably why he did not include it in the *Collected
Poems.*) What poetry now means to Crispin has something to do
with what Stevens here refers to as "the poetry of the thing."

Stevens never called *The Comedian as the Letter C* autobiographical. He refers to it as a life story, but not of Wallace Stevens
in particular.

The long and short of it is simply that I deliberately took the sort
of life that millions of people live, without embellishing it except
by the embellishments in which I was interested at the moment:
words and sounds (*L*, 293).

. . . The central figure is an every-day man who lives a life without
the slightest adventure except that he lives it in a poetic atmosphere
as we all do. . . . (*L*, 778)

We can see throughout the *Collected Poems* that Crispin's
preoccupations are also Stevens' preoccupations. At the time of
his death, Stevens' published opus was the *Collected Poems* and
The Necessary Angel, with no gloss, no theory or explanation in
support of his way of writing poems. The explanations he gives
in his letters are always in response to a specific question about a
poem, or some more general topic connected with poetry. The
explanations usually direct his correspondents back to the poem:
he reminds them that "explanations spoil things" (*L*, 204), and
that "a poem must make its own way" (*L*, 277). These letters,
moreover, were mostly for private use: Stevens gives nothing

outside the poems to either help with the poems or to suggest that they are connected to concerns outside of the poem's particular subject—politics, family life, making a living. When such concerns are introduced, they are put at the service of some theme in poetry. Considering all the opportunities Stevens had in his life to change the way he presented his poems, we can safely assume that he did not want to encourage anyone to pursue these connections. This was not, for him, where the interest of the poems lay.

For one thing, he cherished his privacy: he had no interest in writing for the purpose of making psychological disclosures. Stevens' comments to Ronald Lane Latimer are an astute criticism of a whole class of theories and methods that see in poetry the operation of some single, universal principle which defines and explains whatever the theory or method considers important in human nature.

> You ask whether I should continue to write if no one but myself would ever see my work. There is no reason to believe that anyone will ever see any more of my work; you may change your mind about another book. Anyone who has known a number of poets must have been struck by their extraordinary egotism. There is not the slightest doubt that egotism is at the bottom of what a good many poets do. However, there are other theories about that: for instance, there is the theory that writing poetry is a sexual activity. The truth is that egotism is at the bottom of everything everybody does, and that, if some really acute observer made as much of egotism as Freud has made of sex, people would forget a good deal about sex and find the explanation in egotism. I write poetry because I want to write it. We are likely to give many incorrect explanations for what we do instinctively. It is very easy for me to say that I write poetry in order to formulate my ideas and relate myself to the world. That is why I think I write it, though it may not be the right reason. (*L*, 306)

Stevens' conservatism regarding sexual mores is evident in this comment. That conservatism, and Stevens' own statement here, along with the poems and his journals, make it clear that Stevens did not regard poetry as therapy-through-autobiography. Stevens' objection to Freud's ideas about the centrality of sex were not all based on his conservatism. This passage from *Le Monocle de Mon Oncle* suggests that for him it didn't fit with all the facts.

If sex were all, then every trembling hand
Could make us squeak, like dolls, the wished-for words.
But note the unconscionable treachery of fate
That makes us weep, laugh, grunt, and groan, and shout
Doleful heroics, pinching gestures forth
From madness or delight, without regard
To that first, foremost law. (CP, 13)

His dislike of the idea of "egotism" (evident, I think, in the slight testiness of his comments here) is a sensitive person's response upon recognizing a logical trap. How would Stevens defend his work against a psychologist's statement that it was all motivated by some structural deficiency in his emotional and intellectual makeup? Say, sexual inhibitions that make him obscure, ironic, given to religious yearnings and a love of the sounds of words. Any simple denial of such a motive becomes psychologically suspect also. It's a perverse twist on the "liar's paradox" of philosophers. In bringing up the possibility that Stevens' writing serves the aims of self-assertion, Latimer has (without malice, probably) put him in the position of having to prove a negative. If Stevens writes out of egotism, then the significance of his work, its value, is tied to that egotism, and not in any important way to the importance and interest of the subject matter of the work. Stevens deflects the difficulties that Latimer's question presents by accepting the idea of egotism as a basic motivation, but in such a way that it becomes insignificant: "egotism is at the bottom of everything everybody does." It may be true that Stevens' egotism makes him want to write; but it means no more here than if it made him, or anyone, want to tinker with cars or play golf instead. Stevens recognizes that "egotism" as Latimer uses it means something different, it's a part of a pseudo-scientific theory of human motivation, and as such is interchangeable with the idea of sex as a universally applicable motive, and he doesn't like it much better, except when he has buffered it down to meaning that healthy self-love which Voltaire (in the *Philosophical Dictionary*) says we need in order to take an interest in our lives and our occupations.

But Stevens goes further; in admitting to the possibility that the reasons he has given for writing may be incorrect, he is being candid about the tentativeness of his ideas; they are not static but evolve in ways that he cannot fully anticipate.

Certain passages in Stevens' own life feature in *The Comedian*, but Stevens has put them there for what they tell about "the lives millions of people live." (This description is not all modesty, as we shall see later in this chapter.) Stevens didn't go to Yucatan but he went to Florida and Cuba, and we know from *Harmonium* how fertile in new images he found those places. He had a friend in the South (Judge Powell). He settled in the North, and he got married and had one daughter to Crispin's four. All these occasions differ in their order in the poem and in Stevens' life. Other important factual differences besides the chronological ones mean that discrepancies do not work against the thought that Stevens develops in the poem. The facts of his personal life are inessential. It does not necessarily follow that Stevens will keep all of his personal self out of *The Comedian* or his other poems, or that biographical information about Stevens can never be interesting or relevant. It's simply that we can't treat this information, when we come across it in the poems, as implying that Stevens was a "romantic" poet.[3] As we have seen in *The Comedian as the Letter C*, the first thing that happens to Crispin is the overthrow of that very conception of himself.

When Crispin, newly arrived in Yucatan, surveys the changes that he has undergone, he discovers the new restlessness that is only relieved by writing "the fables that he scrawled / With his own quill, in its indigenous dew" (*CP*, 31). Unlike the "Mayan sonneteers" who have not had any revolution in their thinking— and who have no business writing sonnets in the first place, the

sonnet having come out of Mediterranean, not Mayan culture—
Crispin is not confined any more by narrow notions of what is
the proper subject of poetry. His ideas no longer prevent him
from seeing possibilities in his immediate surroundings. Crispin,
investigating these new possibilities, is fascinated by the details,
by how very different nature is from how he has been used to
think of it.

> The fabulous and its intrinsic verse
> Came like two spirits parleying, adorned
> In radiance from the Atlantic coign,
> For Crispin and his quill to catechize.
> But they came parleying of such an earth,
> So thick with sides and jagged tops of green,
> So intertwined with serpent-kin encoiled
> Among the purple tufts, the scarlet crowns,
> Scenting the jungle in their refuges,
> So streaked with yellow, blue and green and red
> In beak and bud and fruity gobbet-skins,
> That earth was like a jostling festival
> Of seeds grown fat, too juicily opulent,
> Expanding in the gold's maternal warmth. (CP, 32)

In this remarkable passage, Stevens brings together visual elements of the tropical landscape; the colors, the tangle of forms,
"the purple tufts, the scarlet crowns," all blending into one
another except where some odd color or violently broken line
momentarily arrest the attention, "jagged lops of green"; it all
reproduces the chaos of forms that are too big, too bright, too
weird, of sounds too loud and too harsh. This profusion of forms,
as it appears to him, is beyond the domain of any traditional
aesthetic. This passage, as "In the Clear Season of Grapes",
celebrates the discovery of a landscape that is not saturated with
old ideas, indeed will not accommodate them, because of the
violence it does to their dignity. Stevens delights in this excess
and violence and incongruity of the tropical landscape. "Floral

Decorations for Bananas" contrasts a traditional with a tropical aesthetic.

> You should have had plums tonight,
> In an eighteenth-century dish,
> And pettifogging buds,
> For the women of primrose and purl,
> Each one in her decent curl.
> Good God! What a precious light!
>
> But bananas hacked and hunched . . .
> The table was set by an ogre,
> His eye on an outdoor gloom
> And a stiff and noxious place.
> Pile the bananas on planks.
> The women will be all shanks
> And bangles and slatted eyes.
>
> And deck the bananas in leaves
> Plucked from the Carib trees,
> Fibrous and dangling down,
> Oozing cantankerous gum
> Out of their purple maws,
> Darting out of their purple craws
> Their musky and tingling tongues. (CP, 53–54)

The speaker's impatience with "pettifogging buds" and "the women of primrose and purl" changes through the last two stanzas into zest for the grotesque. He quickly sizes up the former and then is drawn to the tropical plants and leaves whose vitality so much resembles that of some weird creature with decidedly non-human intelligence: "The table was set by an ogre." Vegetable forms of the tropics, in their looks and their aggressiveness, begin to seem like animals. But these are animals described in terms of appetite and movement, not in terms of the way they correspond to customary ideas of "the beautiful." The look of the tropical landscape, lacking manners and violating every principle of good taste and decorum, parodies the idea of an aesthetic experience of nature. And like an ogre it is dangerous. During his explorations in Yucatan Crispin finds not only a strange new beauty but also inhuman nature as destructive power. Hearing the storm's approach,

> . . . . Crispin, here, took flight.
> An annotator has his scruples, too.
> He knelt in the cathedral with the rest,
> This connoisseur of elemental fate,
> Aware of exquisite thought. (CP, 32)

The dangers of the tropics set a limit on how much he can do there. He hears in the storm "the span / Of force, the quintessential fact, the note / Of Vulcan." But he himself is in the church, as good a place as any for thinking about his humanity and rediscovering a self that continues to exist separate from nature.

Crispin's adventures so far have resulted from a mixture of vision and circumstance. No explanation is offered for his sudden curiosity about the dolphins. This curiosity takes Crispin further than he intended or even imagined. His encounter with the sea is experience that alters his ideas about poetry, experience that then must be said to alter what poetry *is* or might be. His new ideas about poetry themselves illuminate experiences for him, as for example when he sees new possibilities in the tropics. The storm that sends Crispin into the cathedral for shelter doesn't give him hypotheses so much as it gives him an opportunity for reflection and the impetus to get up and go somewhere else. The storm does not directly cause Crispin's rediscovery of himself: it facilitates it. There are many varieties of causal relationships that make up the circumstances of Cripin's life. Stevens' reflections on life in the poem involve a certain acknowledgment of contingency; when Crispin sets out with a particular intention, it involves him in much that he could not anticipate or prevent. In this respect *The Comedian* stands out as Stevens' only poem that achieves anything like the narrative complexity of a novel. It can be put in a category with novels of coming-of-age—*The Red and the Black*, *A Sentimental Education*, *Tom Jones*, *Sons and Lovers*— and it also resembles Wordsworth's *Prelude*. One doesn't need a magic key to unlock what is hidden behind the sea or the tropics or the northern climates. Things and places may symbolize something; they may stand for all types of experience that bring about these effects on Crispin's character—but nonetheless if we look around in life for examples of these types of experience, the sea, tropical vegetation, and northern winter themselves exemplify the qualities and forces that affect Crispin.

Stevens knows the difference between literal and allegorical. "Anecdote of the Jar" relies on the difference (*CP*, 76). The standard reading of this poem is best articulated by A. Walton Litz: ". . . [A]n artificial form inserted into the 'slovenly wilderness' acts as a catalyst and tames the disorder of nature. The colorless jar, 'gray and bare,' is a sterile and almost menacing object, but . . . it becomes the focus of order (Litz, 92).

Bates and Richardson hold more or less the same view. Bates writes: "Stevens, as his 'Anecdote of the Jar' (1919) indicates, was sufficiently middle-class [middle-class as opposed to what?] to appreciate what is sacrificed when art gains the upper hand" (Bates, 92). Richardson, in a rather curious twist, makes Stevens himself the jar, but perhaps even more curious, it's the same reading: " 'Anecdote of the Jar' . . . has as its controlling image the 'jar' that, in one sense, Stevens felt himself to be in nature . . . and in his own nature, exiled as he was from the possibility of expressing emotions directly. . . . The power of the jar . . . is that of the abstract" (Richardson, 1986, 122). Abstractions, all "gray and bare" as Richardson reminds us in Stevens' phrase, are bad. Joseph Carroll's very close reading concludes: "The jar in the Tennessee represents a purely formal principle of order, and this kind of order cannot satisfy the deepest needs of Stevens' imagination" (Carroll, 37).

Stevens describes the appearance of the jar, its color and symmetry, its bareness. These qualities suggest a sterile orderliness in opposition to the "slovenly wilderness."

The jar is a presence.

Anecdote of the Jar

I placed a jar in Tennessee,
And round it was, upon a hill.
It made the slovenly wilderness
Surround that hill.

The wilderness rose up to it,
And sprawled around, no longer wild.
The jar was round upon the ground
And tall and of a port in air.

It took dominion everywhere.
The jar was gray and bare.
It did not give of bird or bush,
Like nothing else in Tennessee. (CP, 76)

The wilderness is another type of presence, and Tennessee is a place with a certain look to it. It makes a difference in a place when you introduce into it an object that obviously does not belong there. The jar takes dominion everywhere because in a wilderness its form would tend to attract attention, just as a beer can or an old carpet might.

> The wilderness is slovenly after it has been dominated and not before; it "sprawled around, no longer wild." The jar is the product of the human mind, as the critics remark, and it dominates the wilderness; but it does not give order to the wilderness—it is vulgar and sterile, and it transforms the wilderness into the semblance of a deserted picnic ground. (Winters, 437)

If the jar is a focus of order, it is of an unwelcome, unnatural order. If the poem's narrative tells a story that could be true, then our reading of the poem has to include the understanding that the jar is no more of a symbol than a jar can possibly be. A jar, as opposed to, say, a cross or a heap of stones, a flag, or a newly planted tree does not lend itself to symbolism very readily because there doesn't seem to be any way to answer the question, "But why a jar?" Perhaps Stevens chose to write about the jar precisely because it doesn't make a good symbol of anything, except for certain qualities of jar-ness. We approach the poem with our tendencies, as readers, to think in terms of highly general abstractions—order, abstraction—but the abstractions we can arrive at in this case tend to bring us back to the concrete objects we started with because our sense of proportion doesn't let us stray too far. The poem is an anecdote, and anecdotes deal in instances. Stevens was suspicious of his own tendency to abstraction.

> Your question whether art is to a greater or lesser extent didactic is another fundamental question. It might even be said to be the initial question in any aesthetic catechism. A good many people think that I am didactic. I don't want to be. My own idea is that my real danger is not didacticism, but abstraction. It may be because the didactic mind reduces the world to principles or uses abstractions. Whether beauty is roused by passion or passion is roused by beauty is pretty much the same thing as the question whether a poem about a natural object is roused by the natural object or whether the natural object is clothed with its poetic characteristics by the poet. While I brush that sort of thing aside, it is not because I am not interested. But I feel very much like the boy whose mother told him to stop sneezing; he replied: "I am not sneezing; it's sneezing me." (*L*, 302)

From this we can see that it's a good idea to start with a literal, unallegorical reading, just to see what can be done with it. The poem may not end there for us; but often it does and with Stevens this very elementary method can be very difficult. In the nineteen pages of *The Comedian as the Letter C* there are thirty-five changes of argument and circumstance. Some of these changes occur haphazardly; some develop when Crispin examines his own ideas. One of the important themes that *Comedian* raises is the variety of ways in which change comes about in a person's mind and life. The theme is discernible less in the development of an argument or theory than in the action of events and in changes of mood. "Life is Motion" is Stevens' title for a short poem in which not much happens and everything happens.

> In Oklahoma,
> Bonnie and Josie,
> Dressed in calico,
> Danced around a stump.
> They cried,
> "Ohoyaho,
> Ohoo" . . .
> Celebrating the marriage
> Of flesh and air. (CP, 83)

Bonnie and Josie are bodies in nature. (I use the term broadly here to include Oklahoma. That also means oil wells and Oral Roberts.) The action of lives is the marriage of flesh and air: the meeting of what Bonnie and Josie are with what is around them. Crispin's life also happens at this junction and grows through time, making its way amidst the existing possibilities. It does not touch all the possibilities: Crispin doesn't ever seem to go through being in love; he just gets married, so that he never undergoes the sorts of changes associated with romantic relationships. *The Comedian*, by keeping aware of the idea of numberless possible circumstances, also manages to be non-didactic. Crispin has many options besides sin and redemption according to various creeds—Freudian, Tolstoyan, Christian, or Marxist.[4] And yet Crispin, when he turns to North America, is looking for a state of being that will somehow engage all of himself.

> The book of moonlight is not written yet
> Nor half begun, but when it is, leave room
> For Crispin, fagot in the lunar fire,
> Who, in the hubbub of his pilgrimage
> Through sweating changes, never could forget

That wakefulness or meditating sleep,
In which the sulky strophes willingly
Bore up, in time, the somnolent, deep songs. (*CP*, 33)

The tropics with their profusion of forms, of forms that almost seem to be in the very act of becoming something else, have done their part to bring him into new, enlarged awareness of objective reality and of himself in relation to it. When Crispin finds "a self possessing him," he becomes more interested in the workings of that self, and his interest in nature is modified correspondingly. There can be no question of being "annotator," inspector, or botanist, at least for the time being.

How many poems he denied himself
In his observant progress, lesser things
Than the relentless contact he desired;
How many sea-masks he ignored; what sounds
He shut out from his tempering ear; what thoughts,
Like jades affecting the sequestered bride;
And what descants, he sent to banishment! (*CP*, 34)

For a while, Crispin swings helplessly between tropical profusion and the cooler north; in his impatience for the self-immolating passion that he seeks, he misses a lot that is potentially interesting but which requires a different kind of attention. Eventually he loses interest: "Moonlight was an evasion, or, if not, / A minor meeting, facile, delicate" (*CP*, 35). Like the moonlight, the spring is too easy, too pretty: "Was gemmy marionette to him that sought / A sinewy nakedness" (*CP*, 36). When Crispin's vessel is borne upriver in Carolina, he is in a curious frame of mind. He has rejected "the moonlight fiction" (*CP*, 36) and the sterility of the purely subjective—the Yucatan and spring. All he has is his yearning self, with no new specific aim to take its place. The river scene impresses itself, unexpectedly, on his senses.

He savored rankness like a sensualist.
He marked the marshy ground around the dock,
The crawling railroad spur, the rotten fence,
Curriculum for the marvelous sophomore.
It purified. It made him see how much
Of what he saw he never saw at all.
He gripped more closely the essential prose
As being, in a world so falsified,
The one integrity for him, the one
Discovery still possible to make,
To which all poems were incident, unless
That prose should wear a poem's guise at last. (CP, 36)

Crispin's glimpse of "the essential prose" under these particular conditions enables him to see that finding it does not depend on any specific location. Reaching "the essential prose" depends on the quality of attention. The note "his soil is man's intelligence" is not a decree: it represents Crispin's having recognized the dependence of poetry on the unpoetic. Spring and moonlight (and mental moonlight) are legitimate though not exclusive subjects for poetry. They can't be the exclusive subjects because poetry has to be nourished by a consciousness of the world in aspects other than those that are obvious or poetically facile. That consciousness is the intelligence of poetry.

Exit the mental moonlight, exit lex,
Rex and principium, exit the whole
Shebang. Exeunt omnes. Here was prose
More exquisite than any tumbling verse:
A still new continent in which to dwell.
What was the purpose of his pilgrimage,
Whatever shape it took in Cripin's mind,
If not, when all is said, to drive away
The shadow of his fellows from the skies,
And, from their stale intelligence released,
To make a new intelligence prevail? (CP, 37)

Nothing illustrates what Crispin has to "drive out of the sky" so well as this passage from Stevens' journal of 1900:

> Tuesday night Livg + I walked up the Boulevard. A delicate, blue night, most gorgeous,— golden stars + the air as fresh and as pure as the air of the moon. I have a great affection for moonlight nights somehow— + could cry "moon, moon, moon," as fast as the world calls "thief" after a villain —What a treasure house of silver and gold they are— + how lovely the planets look in the heavens— Bah—mere words. (*L*, 46)

The inevitability of some expressions—silver, gold, treasure house, fresh, pure—stops Stevens abruptly in the middle of his enthusiasm. He looks at the night sky and sees the hold that this language has on his mind, and its inadequacy for describing his experience in an interesting or revealing way. Stevens was stymied in 1900 by the poverty of this type of "poetic" language; he makes a vigorous attack on it much later in "Last Looks at the Lilacs" (*CP*, 48). The poet whom the speaker addresses as "Caliper" talks too much.

> To what good, in the alleys of the lilacs,
> O Caliper, do you scratch your buttocks
> And tell the divine ingénue, your companion,
> That this bloom is the bloom of soap
> And this fragrance the fragrance of vegetal? (*CP*, 48)

The divine ingénue is not impressed by similes because her attention is directed elsewhere.

> Do you suppose that she cares a tick
> In this hymeneal air, what it is
> That marries her innocence thus,
> So that her nakedness is near,
> Or that she will pause at scurrilous words? (*CP*, 49)

Stevens' description of poetic language as "scurrilous words" suggests something of how successfully he has been able to master a problem that bedevilled him and to treat that problem and place it in an entirely original setting:

> Poor buffo! Look at the lavender
> And look your last and look still steadily,
> And say how it comes that you see
> Nothing but trash and that you no longer feel
> Her body quivering in the Floréal
>
> Toward the cool night and its fantastic star,
> Prime paramour and belted paragon,
> Well-booted, rugged, arrogantly male,
> Patron and imager of the gold Don John,
> Who will embrace her before summer comes. (CP, 49)

The words that come to this poet's mind when he looks at the lilacs are "trash" compared to the reality of "the cool night and its fantastic star," with which the divine ingénue, quivering in the bushes, is having her own blissful liaison. "Caliper" is done for; the encounter between the divine ingénue and the night, "Prime paramour and belted paragon," is a "marriage of flesh and air" from which Caliper's pedantry excludes him. The "new intelligence" that Crispin wants to see will emerge from such a "marriage," he hopes, somehow. From his first encounter with the sea, Crispin has been constant in his pursuit of a vital contact with objective reality as the only authentic source of poetry. He turns from moonlight to the "rankest trivia"—e.g. "Anecdote of the Jar" and "The Emperor of Ice-Cream" —because he knows he won't find crowds of his fellows there. His "fellows" being the "romantic" poets he wanted not to emulate. (When William Rose Benét asked Stevens to name his favorite of his own poems, Stevens replied: "I think I should select . . . the Emperor of Ice Cream. This wears a deliberately commonplace costume, and yet seems to me to contain something of the essential gaudiness of poetry; that is the reason why I like it." [*L*, 263].)

> The more invidious, the more desired:
> The florist asking aid from cabbages,
> The rich man going bare, the paladin
> Afraid, the blind man as astronomer,
> The appointed power unwielded from disdain. (*CP*, 37)

Stevens shows his disdain for the poetic by making use of goofy noises. For instance the "Tum ti-tum, / Ti tum-tum-tum!" of "Ploughing on Sunday" (*CP*, 20), or the single line "Ho! Ho!" in "Depression Before Spring" (*CP*, 63). Bonnie and Josie the dancing Oklahomans crying "Ohoyaho, Ohoo" seem more gawky than poetic. Stevens had the gift of an ear for important sounding nonsense. (His nickname for his daughter was "Princess Wamsutta Percale" [Holly Stevens, 651].) If "The appointed power" is the poet's ability to fit the appropriate tone and language to his subject, then Stevens disdains to use that ability. Bonnie and Josie, in their antics around the stump, are still celebrating a "marriage of flesh and air" that is as real as can be found anywhere. In Spenser's *Epithalamion*, for example. *Le Monocle de Mon Oncle* meditates on age, mortality, and romantic love, but in the poem angels ride mules— "These muleteers are dainty of their way" (*CP*, 15)— and the attitude of the poem to its subject is summed up in these lines:

> An apple serves as well as any skull
> To be the book in which to read a round,
> And is as excellent, in that it is composed
> Of what, like skulls, comes rotting back to ground. (*CP*, 14)

And yet, these important remarks on Crispin's real purpose occupy a parenthetical place in the development of the argument in section IV of *The Comedian*. The whole section takes an unexpected turn from the very opening line, "his soil is man's intelligence"; the thought could be derived from the last lines of section III. In section IV this "laconic phrase" becomes the inspiration for experimenting with the idea of a colony. The language of the poem seems to suggest that Stevens and Crispin don't think much of the idea:

> The torment of fastidious thought grew slack,
> Another, still more bellicose, came on.
> He, therefore, wrote his prolegomena,
> And, being full of the caprice, inscribed
> Commingled souvenirs and prophecies.
> He made a singular collation. Thus:
> The natives of the rain are rainy men. (CP, 37)

Stevens liked the idea that an environment or locale could express itself through the character and art of the people there. "Anecdote of Men by the Thousand" is Stevens' most direct statement in poetry of this "native aesthetic" idea, though he distances himself from it by making the poem the words of someone just overheard.

> The soul, he said, is composed
> Of the external world.
>
> . . .
>
> There are men whose words
> Are as natural sounds
> Of their places
> As the cackle of toucans
> In the place of toucans.
>
> The mandoline is the instrument
> Of a place.
>
> . . .
>
> The dress of a woman of Lhassa,
> In its place,

> Is an invisible element of that place
> Made visible. (CP, 51)

To understand how Stevens could come to believe, at times, that "invisible elements" of a place express themselves through its people, we have to appreciate his feeling for places. In one of his *Adagia* Stevens wrote: "Life is an affair of people not of places. But for me life is an affair of places and that is the trouble" (*OP*, 158). This "adage" is not simply a negative statement: we have only to look at a few of the poems set in Florida, where the environment seems to imply the presence of a peculiar intelligence at work designing the place. The "Infanta Marina"

> . . . made of the motions of her wrist
> The grandiose gestures
> Of her thought.
>
> The rumpling of the plumes
> Of this creature of the evening
> Came to be sleights of sails
> Over the sea. (CP, 7)

In "O Florida, Veneral Soil" the speaker appeals to that almost visible presence. He wants her to disclose to "the lover"

> A few things for themselves,
> Convolvulus and coral,
> Buzzards and live-moss,
> Tiestas from the keys,
> A few things for themselves,
> Florida, venereal soil. . . . (CP, 47)

The disclosure of these "invisible elements made visible" are evidences of a reassuring order and intelligence that exists in spite of and beyond

> The dreadful sundry of this world,
> the Cuban, Polodowsky,
> The Mexican women,
> The negro undertaker
> Killing the time between corpses
> Fishing for crayfish . . . (CP, 47)

which all inhabit Florida the way the jar inhabits Tennessee. In the quiet and shadow of night, when the world slows down and the imagination is not overwhelmed by the distraction of the daylight world, the lover cannot resist the thought of that order.

> Swiftly in the nights,
> In the porches of Key West,
> Behind the bougainvilleas,
> After the guitar is asleep,
> Lasciviously as the wind,
> You come tormenting,
> Insatiable . . . (CP, 48)

In these poems we can see how he associates certain forms that appear in a specific place—in this case, Florida—with this invisible presence. If Florida's landscape can seem to imply a local intelligence or order, then it is easy to see how attractive the idea would be to Stevens if he could apply it more broadly as a program for getting at the truly native. It is the satisfaction of the "inchling" in "Bantams in Pine-Woods" (CP, 75) that he can say to the ten-foot poet, "Your world is you. I am my world" (CP, 75). Thus, in *The Comedian*:

> The man in Georgia walking among pines
> Should be pine-spokesman. The responsive man,
> Planting his pristine cores in Florida,
> Should prick thereof, not on the psaltery,
> But on the banjo's categorical gut,
> Tuck, tuck, while the flamingoes flapped his bays.

Sepulchral señors, bubbling pale mescal,
Oblivious to the Aztec almanacs,
Should make the intricate Sierra scan.
And dark Brazilians in their cafes,
Musing immaculate, pompean dits,
Should scrawl a vigilant anthology. (CP, 38)

Soon enough, though, Crispin is "irked beyond his patience" by
the confinement of living within a predetermined artistic program. Crispin comes to understand the inherent weakness of
such programs by experience. Thus, he begins with an idea that
in some visionary moments appears to him as an essential,
enlightening fact about experience. The Florida ladies and ideas
of order are powerful intuitions; at the time these intuitions
occur, they persuasively suggest descriptions of the world—"The
dress of a woman of Lhassa / . . . Is an invisible element of that
place / Made visible"—that offer the possibility to him of transcendence or harmony. At such moments of intuition we can say
that he sees the prospect before him of a world that is ordered
and purposeful, but which also promises imaginative interplay
between himself and it, that is even richer than what he is
experiencing at the moment. At this stage, and as long as
interesting possibilities present themselves, the idea naturally
attracts him. It works for him; he can use it. The sketch he makes
of the possibilities is itself an interesting poem.

But from the moment Crispin sets his idea above his head as
a prescription for his art, he runs into difficulties. His allegiance
is divided; he cannot produce to order poems that have the
authority of "the essential prose," and he does not care to falsify.
His position resembles that of a painter of the thirties, someone
who becomes persuaded that he has a political commitment to
realism or localism; even though he has a social conscience he
may be bored to distraction by the subject and the demands it
makes on his sense of his medium. Such a painter may feel that
the class struggle is more important than his own tentative (or
impulsive) explorations into uncertainty, and then perhaps he

would submit. Or he may abandon the class struggle and his
boredom and become some kind of renegade, doubtful character
who may or may not make something wonderful. Crispin's
program is his own invention of course, and there is no suggestion that he has shared it with anyone else; but in his own mind
it dictates what he should devote his energies to.[5] It places him
in a relation to his experience that resembles the old Crispin: a
man whose art is defined by a fixed (unexamined, exempt from
criticism) ideology. He would be writing his "couplet yearly to
the spring" again, cut off from great tracts of experience.

> . . . . Hence it was,
> Preferring text to gloss, he humbly served
> Grotesque apprenticeship to chance event,
> A clown, perhaps, but an aspiring clown. (CP, 39)

He abandons his artistic program, and as a consequence his
poetry now cannot claim the special kind of justification of being
aligned with some aim for the improvement of human life.
Presumably, if the program had been successfully carried out,
the man in Georgia, the sepulchural señors and the dark Brazilians would all be happier with their art than they had been
before. This is the closest Crispin gets to having a public agenda,
and when he rejects it, he is refusing to use himself or his
abilities as the instrument of an ideology, even if it is his own,
and even if it is an ideology whose aims are still only artistic.

> Trinket pasticcio, flaunting skyey sheets,
> With Crispin as the tiptoe cozener?
> No, no: veracious page on page, exact. (CP, 40)

Crispin has fallen out with two of the most respectable justifica-
tions for writing poetry: the first, the romantic role of the poet as
"the Socrates / Of snails" which would be continuous with
tradition; the second, the program for the reform of poetry, in
which his creations would serve an aim different from their own

development (or nondevelopment): namely, the aim of the improvement of living conditions—in this case the living conditions of poetry.

Crispin's status as a poet, without these definitions, becomes very uncertain. What is to distinguish him, as a poet, from ordinary people around him? He's no longer a man with a mission. He's a man with a private life; in the place he happens to be in, "Crispin as hermit, pure and capable / Dwelt in the land." This phrase is repeated:

> Crispin dwelt in the land and dwelling there
> Slid from his continent by slow recess
> To things within his actual eye. . . . (*CP*, 40)

Crispin's range of vision narrows. Until now he has had his eye on continents—broad areas in which particulars have equal value. He has had a generalized, bird's-eye view of his experience, and his thinking has tended to work itself out in abstractions. Throughout Crispin's adventures we have seen him motivated by abstract qualities that inhere in certain locales, then come to an even more generalized form of abstraction. But he has not been stuck anywhere; he has not had any commitments, no attachments to unique objects. This is the last major change he undergoes.

> It seemed haphazard denouement.
> He, first, as realist, admitted that
> Whoever hunts a matinal continent
> May, after all, stop short before a plum
> And be content and still be realist.
> The words of things entangle and confuse.
> The plum survives its poems. It may hang
> In the sunshine placidly, colored by ground
> Obliquities of those who pass beneath,
> Harlequined and mazily dewed and mauved

In bloom. Yet it survives in its own form,
Beyond these changes, good, fat, guzzly fruit. (CP, 41)

Crispin's "sinking" from public to private life has generally been considered the defeat of his poetic ambitions. His whole enterprise, according to some critics, ends in failure or in the renunciation of poetry. The uncertainty into which Crispin enters, though, is a transformation as potentially radical as his sea voyage. Yvor Winters saw the renunciation of poetry as the virtually inescapable conclusion of Crispin's undertaking.

> In the fifth and sixth parts, Crispin's concentration upon the normal world about him results in his marrying and begetting daughters; and finding that the facts which he had set out to describe with such exemplary honesty are more engrossing than the description of them, he abandons his art, in order, as very young people are sometimes heard to say, to live. This is not surprising for the honest description which Crispin set out to achieve is in itself a moral experience, though of a very limited kind: honest description renders the feeling appropriate to purely sensory experience. But if Crispin had realized this, he would have realized the whole moral basis of art, and would have proceeded to more complex subjects; not realizing this, he lost interest in his simplified art, and found the art even in this simplified form to be the last element of confusion remaining in his experience. (Winters, 442)

(It's worth noting, in passing, that Winters' discussion of the passage quoted above omits the image of the plum hanging "In the sunshine placidly, colored by ground / Obliquities of those who pass beneath, / Harlequined and mazily dewed. . . ." The plum has two lives of which Crispin may be aware: its life "in its own form," as "good, fat, guzzly fruit," and its existence as worked upon by the imagination of people and by its situation, its living so near this stream of traffic. This complication of the existence of an object, we know, fascinated Stevens: we can infer from his introduction of it here that it will be an essential part of all Crispin's future encounters with objects.)

Crispin's "haphazard denouement" brings him to a state of being not "Everyman" but just like everybody else. Milton J. Bates puts it happily: "He would seem, finally, to be the intelligence only of his own intelligence" (Bates, 119). The renunciation of poetry is an act directed against poetry—or at least against certain familiar rationalizations for poetry—but it is also an act of *choice* of experience unmediated by poetry as he has developed it until now. Poetry now has to compete among his other interests and commitments which are such as evolve naturally in human life, and if it survives, the possibility exists that that poetry will have the authenticity he has sought all along. Crispin has had to renounce his life on the "continental" scale in favor of a life, as Stevens might have put it, on the scale of the normal. His poetry will not sustain itself at a "higher" level of generalization. But one of the conditions of this new life for his poetry is an absolute uncertainty as to its status and future. This is an objective fact as intransigent as a plum; Crispin cannot, therefore, use the romantic or any of his various poetic voices to decry the condition to which poetry and himself have been reduced.

> Was he to bray this in profoundest bass
> Anointing his dreams with fugal requiems?
> Was he to company vastest things defunct
> With a blubber of tom-toms harrowing the sky?
> . . .
> Should he lay by the personal and make
> Of his own fate an instance of all fate?
> What is one man among so many men?
> What are so many men in such a world?
> Can one man think one thing and think it long?
> Can one man be one thing and be it long? (*CP*, 41)

This passage is not a complaint; it is a realization. It is the moment when Crispin becomes truly naive again, in the sense used by Baudelaire. Treating experience as experience, and not as fodder for poetry, or as something that cannot be evaded in poetry. Thus poetry is obliged to make its way among the objective conditions in which it finds itself, here, now. Winters' criticism of this part of *The Comedian*, that Crispin gives up on "honest description" of "purely sensory experience," and his contention that Stevens did not have the courage to renounce poetry, seems partly a reaction against Stevens' language, and against Stevens' (to Winters) preference for simple, "purely sensory experience." As we have seen, Stevens did not think of "purely sensory experience" as simple in the way that Winters seems to mean. But then, Winters had no way of knowing some of the things Stevens said about the proper place for poetry in relation to life. In a long letter to Harvey Breit, Stevens took great pains to dismiss the notion that his life as a poet was in some way deeply divided from his life as an executive of the Hartford Accident and Indemnity Company. What that could mean is perhaps most charmingly expressed by a former colleague at the Hartford: "I don't think he was particularly keen about somebody kowtowing to him, and I certainly never did. I just took him as I found him. I tried to respect his wishes, but I used to let him have it a little bit because he was just another damn poet. In my book, he wasn't John Keats" (Brazeau, 44).

Crispin is not sure that he is even a poet anymore, he doesn't know if he is different from anyone else:

> As a matter of fact, the conception of poetry itself has changed and is changing every day. Poetry is a thing that engages, or should engage, not the human curiosities to whom you referred, but men of serious intelligence. I think that every poet of any interest considers himself as a person concerned with something essential and vital. That such a person is to be visualized as "an idler, a man without clothes, a drunk" or in any way as an eccentric or a person somehow manqué is nonsense. The contemporary poet is simply a contemporary man who writes poetry. He looks like anyone else, acts like anyone else, wears the same kind of clothes, and is certainly not an incompetent. (*L*, 413.)

Winters would not have known, either, about Stevens' *Adagia*. Stevens liked adages and aphorisms and had a large collection of them. He liked to write them himself; the whole range of his ideas appears in them. Some of his *Adagia* may be statements of convictions; but it is safer and no less effective to treat them as propositions he tried out, working hypotheses. The selection I make here does not represent Stevens' only thought on this subject; it only shows that he thought about it in this particular way and came back to it more than once.

> To live in the world but outside of existing conceptions of it. (*OP*, 164)
> It is not every day that the world arranges itself into a poem. (*OP*, 165)
> The great conquest is the conquest of reality. It is not enough to present life, for a moment, as it might have been. (*OP*, 168)
> The poem reveals itself only to the ignorant man. (*OP*, 160)
> The fundamental difficulty in any art is the problem of the normal. (*OP*, 169)
> Consider: I. That the whole world is material for poetry; II. That there is not a specifically poetic material. (*OP*, 162)
> A man cannot search life for unprecedented experiences. (*OP*, 172)
> Poetry is a response to the daily necessity of getting the world right. (*OP*, 176)

These adages suggest something of what Stevens intends when he calls Crispin a "realist." A realist accepts commitments, attachments, wife, daughters, domestic comfort, and the unsolicited pleasures of nature that dispel his poetic discontent, all as part of the organic conditions of life. Poetry makes its way in these conditions, and if it fails, then poetry is not workable. This is the meaning of the line "For realist, what is is what should be"

84   Wallace Stevens

(*CP*, 41). It does not have anything to do with the optimism
Voltaire satirized in *Candide*:

> "Well! My dear Pangloss," said Candide, "when you were
> hanged, dissected, stunned with blows and made to row in the
> galleys, did you always think that everything was for the best in this
> world?"
> "I am still of my first opinion," replied Pangloss, "for after all
> I am a philosopher . . . " (Voltaire, 321)

though Stanley Burnshaw attacked it as having that sense: "Realists have been bitter at the inanity of Pope's 'Whatever is, is right,'
but Stevens plunges ahead to the final insolence: 'For realists,
what is is what should be' (Burnshaw, 36).[6]

Pope was not a metaphysician; Pangloss was a bad one.
Neither Crispin nor Candide make any pretensions to being
metaphysicians, preferring Socratic ignorance— "I know that I
do not know." Candide can happily and responsibly ignore his
metaphysical uncertainty; Crispin lives in its atmosphere.

> Crispin concocted doctrine from the rout.
> The world, a turnip once so readily plucked,
> Sacked up and carried overseas, daubed out
> Of its ancient purple, family font,
> The same insoluble lump. The fatalist
> Stepped in and dropped the chuckling down his craw,
> Without grace or grumble. (*CP*, 45)

We do not know at the end of *The Comedian* whether Crispin's
fatalism is a successful conclusion to his adventures. (Candide's
is, by definition.)

> . . . if the music sticks, if the anecdote
> Is false, if Crispin is a profitless
> Philosopher, beginning with green brag,
> Concluding fadedly, if as a man
> Prone to distemper he abates in taste,

Fickle and fumbling, visible, obscure,
Glozing his life with after-shining flicks,
Illuminating, from a fancy gorged
By apparition, plain and common things,
Sequestering the fluster from the year,
Making gulped potions from obstreperous drops,
And so distorting, proving what he proves
Is nothing, what can all this matter since
The relation comes benignly to its end? (CP, 46)

"The central figure is an every-day man who lives a life without
the slightest adventure except that he lives it in a poetic atmosphere as we all do. . . ." (L, 778).

Chapter Four

S tevens once remarked to a correspondent that "While poems may very well occur, they had very much better be caused" (*L*, 274). Poems can be made to look as though they occurred, and a poem that is made may still contain much that occurs.

We need not assume that because most of Stevens' poems (and especially *Harmonium*) do not follow an explicitly stated program, they are not inherently as important as a poem, like *Notes toward a Supreme Fiction*, that does have a program. The failed "Mr. Burnshaw and the Statue" is an instance of a poem with a program. The success or failure of a poem is not simply a matter of how well it carries out a program: the program itself is an issue. Marjorie Perloff, who has reservations about the program of *Notes*, rightly wonders at the way some writers on Stevens have embraced it without any reservations at all (Perloff, 1985, 57). Stevens himself, as we have seen in *The Comedian*, knew that difficulties arose out of the conflict between an artistic program and reality, though the knowledge did not prevent him from becoming fascinated, and imaginatively stimulated for a time, by the idea of the "supreme fiction." (A lot of time had passed, to be sure—plenty of opportunity for the workings of contingency again.) The merit of *Notes* or of any of the later, more ambitious poems still depends on how much they comprehend the conditions of their creation and on how that comprehension is expressed as poetry. Does *Notes toward a Supreme Fiction* resolve or restate the uncertainties that we see at the end of *The Comedian as the Letter C*, or has it simply forgotten them?

Harmonium gives a standard by which one can evaluate the achievement of *Notes*, and of course it works the other way too— or at least it should.

Crispin's adventure is that of a poet who has been more or less stuck with writing poetry in the terms set by the tradition as he finds it, until his experience of the actual world and of his own self makes it necessary for him to change. His sea voyage and the revelations of Yucatan are two important, transforming moments. Another is his trip upriver into Carolina.

As he travels upriver, he notices the distinct character of the river landscape.

> Tilting up his nose,
> He inhaled the rancid resin, burly smells,
> Of dampened lumber, emanations blown
> From warehouse doors, the gustiness of ropes,
> Decays of sacks, and all the arrant stinks
> That helped him round his rude aesthetic out.
> He savored rankness like a sensualist.
> He marked the marshy ground around the dock,
> The crawling railroad spur, the rotten fence. . . . (CP, 36)

It impresses him unexpectedly; it "made him see how much / Of what he saw he never saw at all" (*CP*, 36). Here is another of Stevens' peculiar negatives, like his "nothing that is not there and the nothing that is." Seeing, Crispin discovers again, involves also not seeing. The old Crispin thought he knew the sun to be one of the civilized comforts of his little world, but his time at sea taught him that the sun's existence outside of his idea of it was a very different thing: ". . . the sun / Was not the sun because it never shone / With bland complaisance on pale parasols . . ." (*CP*, 29).

Human life is no more to the sun than the parasol is to human life. Crispin has learned about scale. On the river, too, he finds that his vision, even at the level of his own immediate experience, has been circumscribed by a point of view, an aesthetic judgment that values certain experiences excessively (moonlight, spring), and ignores others (rancid resin, old newspapers, deal tables missing glass knobs). Stevens criticized this point of view in some remarks on his poem "Sailing After Lunch" (*CP*, 120).

> When people speak of the romantic, they do so in what the French commonly call a *pejorative* sense. But poetry is essentially romantic, only the romantic of poetry must be something constantly new and, therefore, just the opposite of what is spoken of as the romantic. Without this new romantic, one gets nowhere; with it, the most casual things take on transcendence, and the poet rushes brightly, and so on. What one is always doing is keeping the romantic pure: eliminating from it what people speak of as the romantic. (*L*, 277)

"What people speak of as the romantic" is also attacked in "Last Looks at the Lilacs." This romantic is what Stevens had to contend with: it had absorbed so many traditional forms—ballads, sonnets, tales, odes—and, at best, "modernized" them in a way not unlike the way Pope "modernized" Donne and Chaucer. At worst, it presented them as kitsch. Even the way old poems were presented, and the ones that were preferred, as evident in anthologies like *Palgrave's Golden Treasury*, reflected an attitude about what was good in poems. This was one reason why Pound loathed the *Golden Treasury*.

The poetry of spring is indeed a "gemmy marionette" (CP, 36) to Crispin when he realizes that he has lost sight of the original reason for taking it up, and that the writing itself is in a manner for which the original justification no longer exists. Crispin lost sight of the reasons because he was living inside of what he did not know was a conventional view of both the world and himself. A "gemmy marionette" is a nice thing, of course, it is everything a poem can be according to the conventions. It is an aesthetic object like the fruit on the table in "In the Clear Season of Grapes"; its very status as poetry renders it trivial and artificial. This is also the condition of spring in "The Man on the Dump."

> The freshness of night has been fresh a long time.
> The freshness of morning, the blowing of day, one says
> That it puffs as Cornelius Nepos reads, it puffs
> More than, less than or it puffs like this or that.
> The green smacks in the eye, the dew in the green
> Smacks like fresh water in a can, like the sea
> On a cocoanut—how many men have copied dew
> For buttons, how many women have covered themselves
> With dew, dew dresses, stones and chains of dew, heads
> Of the floweriest flowers dewed with the dewiest dew.
> One grows to hate these things except on the dump.
>   (CP, 201)

It's not that spring or moonlight have ceased to be interesting experiences, but that in the way they have been written about, in their traditional characters, they do not speak to Crispin in his search for the "sinewy nakedness" (CP, 36) that is more human, more true to the way he is. In "The Man on the Dump" Stevens finds a way to talk about spring and moonlight that suits his concerns.

> Now, in the time of spring (azaleas, trilliums,
> Myrtle, viburnums, daffodils, blue phlox),

Between that disgust and this, between the things
That are on the dump (azaleas and so on)
And those that will be (azaleas and so on),
One feels the purifying change. One rejects
The trash.

     That's the moment when the moon creeps up
To the bubbling of bassoons. That's the time
One looks at the elephant-colorings of tires.
Everything is shed; and the moon comes up as the moon
(All its images are in the dump) and you see
As a man (not like an image of a man),
You see the moon rise in the empty sky. (*CP*, 202)

This moon rises accompanied by the sound of a new kind of
music (or at least an old musical instrument put to a new use):
something different from a lute or an Aeolian harp. It casts its
light on the "elephant-colorings" of tires. To continue to uncrit-
ically use the junk of imagery and metaphor, the flowers and
dew-creations, is to fail to be conscious of the dump—the
unpoetic, "the wrapper on the can of pears / the cat in the paper
bag"— and of the true character of yourself "As a man (not an
image of a man)" —and of the bareness beyond yourself and the
dump, the bareness of the moon and the empty sky. It means
being unable to distinguish between received ideas and the reality
around you. The poet can use any instrument he wants to get at
his subject, but to persist in producing with forms that have
outlived their usefulness comes to look like ridiculous posturing
and self-deceit. Of course, nothing absolutely outlives its usefulness. Anything can be picked up off the dump of discarded forms
and put to a new use.

One sits and beats an old tin can, lard pail.
One beats and beats for that which one believes.
That's what one wants to get near.
  . . .

. . . . Is it peace,
Is it a philosopher's honeymoon, one finds
On the dump? Is it to sit among mattresses of the dead,
Bottles, pots, shoes and grass and murmur *aptest eve:*
Is it to hear the blatter of grackles and say
Invisible priest; is it to eject, to pull
The day to pieces and cry *stanza my stone?*
Where was it one first heard of the truth? The the. (CP, 203)

As I have pointed out before, Crispin has not really been
expecting that rank experience of the most unpoetic sort should
get him thinking in a serious way again. It makes him choose
between his previous aesthetic attitude and what is offered by
"the essential prose" (CP, 36). He chooses the "essential prose"
because of the poverty of romanticism in the state in which he
finds it, and because its exclusiveness falsifies the world by not
telling the truth about experience, part of the neglected truth
being that what he finds on the river is important. It's important
because it gives him a kind of pleasure: "He savored rankness like
a sensualist" (CP, 36).

He gripped more closely the essential prose
As being, in a world so falsified
The one integrity for him, the one
Discovery still possible to make,
To which all poems were incident, unless
That prose should wear a poem's guise at last. (CP, 36)

Stevens is using the word "incident" in the sense defined as
follows in the Oxford English Dictionary: "occurring or liable to
occur by the way, or in the course of something else of which it
has no essential part." The "essential prose" is simply the truth.
The possibility that poetry can be the truth gets Crispin interested
in poetry again. He has discovered for himself what Sir Philip
Sidney means in the *Apology for Poetry* when he speaks of the
poet as "having all, from Dante's heaven to his hell, under the

authority of his pen" (Sidney, 225). The landscapes that Crispin has hitherto excluded from his vision tell him not only about themselves but also about the world and the way he sees it. The river landscape is not significant simply because it is ugly and "anti-poetic" but because it gives Crispin an unsought and unanticipated insight. That alone may not make it the truth, but it is certainly not just another creation of his "poetic" vision. Crispin does not "affirm," to use Sidney's word, that seedy places are the only ones where real life can be found; his glimpse of these places enables him to judge his old poetic ideas by a more comprehensive range of values and possibilities.

Crispin's choice of the truth ultimately means that he lives with uncertainty about the future and the success of his future artistic endeavors. What he subsequently writes may not be poetry, or it may be "mere" poetry. That is, he may do nothing, or what he does may not pass with other people as poetry, or it may not satisfy his own expectations. Or it may be something new and unique born out of his peculiar vision and circumstances that is recognizable as serious poetry. Having established this high standard of truthfulness, there is nothing he can do *instead*. The poetry that he makes by this standard must work as poetry.

Stevens' art operates with the same type of uncertainty. It is not an uncertainty as to whether he has the initiative or capacity to write good poems: it's an uncertainty about the character of the art itself because of the state of doubt which is necessary to its creation. It was necessary for Stevens to develop a wariness, a protectiveness about his poems. He didn't want explanations to be substituted for what was on the page; he wanted his audience to hear him with the right kind of attention. It is in reference to these conditions that we must interpret the much-quoted statements heading the opening sections of *Notes toward a Supreme Fiction*.

Stevens' life, habits, temperament and poetic ideas kept him separate from the influence of Pound and Eliot. He was on friendly terms with Frost and with Williams, who was surely the only person who gave Stevens advice on the composition of a poem. Advice which Stevens took.

Dear Stevens:
Congratulations on winning ARRIET'S [sic] prize!

I am keeping a copy of "The Worms at Heaven's Gate" which is to my mind a splendid poem. An exchange of letters may be necessary before we agree on the final version of the thing as i [sic] am thoroughly convinced that a change or two will strengthen the poem materially. I have made the changes and given my reasons as inclosed . . .

I have changed line two from
"Within her bellies, as a chariot,"
to the following:
"Within her bellies, we her chariot,"

I think the second version is much the better for the reason that THE WORMS ARE HER CHARIOT and not only seem her chariot. Then again: "bellies" "as a chariot" (plural and singular) sounds badly while "we her chariot" has more of a collective sense and feels more solid. What do you say?

I have left off the last two lines for the obvious reason that they are fully implied in the poem: the lowness of the worms, the highness of Badroulbadour. This is a weakening of the truth of the poem by a sentimental catch at the end.

For Christ's sake yield to me and become great and famous.

Williams[1]

We know that when work for the Hartford did not keep him busy, Stevens led a surprisingly active life in poetry, contributing to magazines, and collaborating in a small way, and at a distance, on a variety of projects with artists in other media. He wrote reviews of the work of Williams, Marianne Moore, and John Crowe Ransom, and he was willing, except insofar as his contract with Alfred Knopf prohibited, to send a poem to just about anybody who asked for one.

He claimed not to know much about Pound. He declined to participate in the symposium "The Case For and Against Ezra Pound." *Harmonium* was published less than a year after *The Waste Land*, which established Eliot for a long time as the major voice of modernism in poetry. Stevens wrote to Richard Eberhart in 1954:

> I am not conscious of having been influenced by anybody and have purposely held off from reading highly mannered people like Eliot and Pound so that I should not absorb anything, even unconsciously. (*L*, 813.)

While the myth of Stevens' isolated life (summarized by Edmund Wilson: "The idea of the Hartford insurance man who has never been abroad but fancies himself as a wistful Pierrot inhabiting the *fin de siecle* I have always found somewhat repellent. . . . [Wilson, 702]) proves to be just a myth, it was nevertheless true that in certain ways Stevens chose not to be in touch. Knowing the influence of the work of Pound and Eliot in criticism as well as in poetry, Stevens deliberately avoided them. He wanted to maintain his own identity separate from them, as Crispin wanted "to drive the shadow of his fellows from the skies" (*CP*, 37). Still, he knew enough about Eliot to be able to say "Eliot and I are dead opposites and I have been doing everything that he would not be able to do" (*L*, 677). He wanted it to be clear that he was going his own way. And certainly at the time when Pound was helping Eliot write *The Waste Land*, and helping everybody else—the time when Pound's ideas were making a big difference in the thinking of Eliot's poetry—Stevens was working on his own.

Against this background it is interesting to place these observations by Litz on currents in Stevens' reputation:

> When Marius Bewley surveyed the existing criticism of Wallace Stevens' poetry in 1949 [seven years after the publication of *Notes Toward a Supreme Fiction*], he discovered a "persistent bias" in favor of Stevens' first volume of verse, *Harmonium* (1923) and a

corresponding neglect of the later work. The poems of *Harmonium* were taken by most readers as the center of Stevens' poetic achieve- ment, and the major poetry which followed *The Man with the Blue Guitar* (1937) had scarcely been assimilated. Today the opposite bias prevails: the later poetry has become the focus of critical attention, and the poetry of 1914–37 is in danger of being arbitrar- ily absorbed into the "grand poem" of the later years. (Litz, v)

He points out that interest in Stevens' late work began to grow from about the early fifties, between the publication of *The Necessary Angel* (1951) and *Opus Posthumous* (1957). The pub- lication of these books (and, of course, *The Collected Poems* in 1954), Litz says, "made evident the coherence and power of Stevens' final 'poetic' " (Litz, v).

Introspective Voyager is an attempt to slow down the bias favoring the later work; Litz concedes that it is "understandable" why the later poems should be more interesting to critics (includ- ing Litz). He doesn't, however, give any kind of account of how the shift took place, or of what motivated it. The initial prefer- ence to *Harmonium* may have been no more well-considered among many of Stevens' readers than the later one has become. (Which is not to say that there aren't many people whose interest in Stevens' work is outside either of these tendencies.) Beginning with the Aiken-Untermeyer controversy, with Untermeyer charg- ing— in response to Aiken's comments on his book *The New Era in American Poetry*—that Stevens' poems (along with those of some other poets) lacked "soul" (Aiken, Untermeyer, 58).

Stanley Burnshaw's criticism of *Ideas of Order* (Burnshaw, 36) took up again the charges that Aiken had not actually refuted, so much as simply said they weren't culpable. Burnshaw's dis- missal of Stevens came from within the Marxist historical dogma[2] even if Stevens' work was more obviously didactic it probably would have been considered "stuck in its time," not relevant to the historical moment.

Even Edmund Wilson's opinion of Stevens' early poetry did not differ much from this general trend: "His early book *Harmo-*

nium has some nice—purely verbal—writing, but his more pretentious stuff bores me. . . ." (Wilson, 702).

Twelve years passed between the publication of *Harmonium* and that of *Ideas of Order*. But it was not until much later that Stevens was thought of by most critics otherwise than as a poet of concrete experience and gaudy word-music; a poet without a theory—a poet you just appreciated.

Longfellow was the only previous American poet to enjoy the fame and acceptance, the welcome into the academy that Eliot received. Eliot was a poet with a theory; with a professed critical consciousness of the history of his art. Stevens (apparently) just naively wrote poems in his strange idiom. With the publication of the later books, however, it became more evident, or at least more widely known, that Stevens did have a method, did have a critical consciousness, different from Eliot's, but equally (arguably better, for that matter) developed.

In the interval between *Ideas of Order* and this recognition there were important exceptions: Winters, Matthieson, Martz, Blackmur, and some of Stevens' fellow-poets, people who were in the know from the beginning; Williams, Allen Tate and others whose names we may never know. There were enough to suggest the existence of a substantial body of people who knew all along that Stevens was thinking hard in *Harmonium*, who knew that his "poetic," as Litz calls it, was developed very early. Litz acknowledges so much when he says that ". . . the best reader of the last volumes is the reader instructed in the earlier poems" (Litz, vi).

It is tempting to think that Stevens became for the later critics the poet that Eliot had been. Marjorie Perloff has written on the question whether the twentieth century will end up belonging to Pound or Stevens (or at least to their disciples) (Perloff, 1982, 485). But this Stevens is not the Stevens of *Harmonium*, except insofar as *Harmonium* has been seen as the precursor of the later works.

It is beyond the scope of this study to examine the later poems in the kind of detail that I have given to *Harmonium*. I

confess to a preference for the earlier poems, though there are
many poems throughout *The Collected Poems* that I like as much.
I have thought that my lack of equal enthusiasm for the currently
more popular poems might mean that there was something I did
not get. I was curious to see how *Harmonium* had been illuminated by what critics had found in the later poems, or even in
the whole body of Stevens' work. The quotations that follow are
the results of a survey taken from some of the principal works of
four leaders of opinion on Stevens.

Frank Kermode:

> *Harmonium* is not without its meditative poems, and it contains in
> the germ a great deal of what might be called the doctrine of
> Stevens, although the word suggests an assertiveness absent from
> his world. But it is true that *Harmonium* is on the whole very much
> more concerned than the later poetry with establishing the con-
> tours, the colours, the fortuity of Stevens' world—with reality
> "arranging itself into poems" of the "gaudiness" necessary to the
> fictive presentation of its own texture, its own strangeness. This is
> its theme, and it is a theme of delight. *Harmonium* has little—but
> not quite nothing—to say of what Stevens later came to call
> "poverty"—meaning the absence of a fruitful union between imag-
> ination and reality. (Kermode, 25)

The "not quite nothing" that *Harmonium* has to say about the
"absence of a fruitful union between imagination and reality"
includes *Sunday Morning, The Comedian as the Letter C*, "The
Snow Man," "The Man Whose Pharynx Was Bad". . . .

Roy Harvey Pearce:

> Stevens tries to spell out the lesson in the longest, most difficult,
> most ambitious, and, I think, most inadequate of the poems in
> *Harmonium, The Comedian as the Letter C*. Here the protagonist,
> condemned, once more, to a life of rich perceptions, is something
> of a poet. Thus he is in a position to reflect learnedly and at length
> on his situation and generally to resolve its meaning. . . .
> Yet its technique is of a kind which can only inhibit the
> emergence of this meaning. Particulars get in the way of implicit

generalization—the sense of detail, however much imaginatively informed, in the way of implicit dialectics. . . . The overplus of language—parallels, appositions, repetitions, words unabsorbed into the whole, the overpowering concreteness, maximally irrelevant texture—gets in the way of the developing analysis of the poet's situation and what it is coming to. The poet-protagonist himself, with his powerful sensibility, gets in the way. (Pearce, 1961, 88)

It would be a formidable task to address the objections this writer has made to the presence of every feature of the poem that distinguishes it from a scholarly article on literary theory; first we would have to adjust our wits to the notion that a person can be "condemned . . . to a life of rich perceptions" (as opposed to blessed with a life of wretched insensibility?).

Helen Vendler:

> *The Comedian as the Letter C* is fantastic in its language and belongs, in the spectrum of poetic effort, at the end where we find anagrams, schemes, acrostics, figure poems, double sestinas, and so on—the poetry of ingenuity, the poetry with overt verbal designs on its readers. At least, that is our first impression. Then we notice that together with the obvious simplicity of the plot we have occasional corresponding simplicities of speech, lulls in the erratic gothic harmonies of the words. These simplicities are of several kinds, just as the coruscations are; together they bound the stylistic extremes of the poem and frame its rhetorical architecture. (Vendler, 1969, 38)

By "simplicities" she means, I take it, those simple, declarative sentences, usually one line, that occasionally interrupt the normal pace of the poem. There is no indication that she is aware of Stevens' having any conscious intention with regard to the style.

She also seems to share Pearce's horror at the thought of a life of rich perception, and is quite sure that Stevens could not possibly have liked living one.

> Stevens felt obliged to pretend an instinct for the fertility of earth, when his true instinct was for its austerities and its dilapidations. Pursuing the *ignis fatuus* of luxuriance, he came to grief, not only

in the poetry of the daughters but in other parts of the *Comedian* as well, where in convulsions of diction violence is done to language by archaism, slang, and affectation all jumbled together. (Vendler, 1969, 45)

Harold Bloom calls this last Vendler's "most telling indictment of Stevens" (Bloom, 76) and says that *Harmonium* is dominated by "the *pathos*, or failed Will-to-Power, of finding the self to be only a mutilated part of a desired wholeness . . ." (Bloom, 76).

The writing of all these critics is so unfocused that it is difficult to be sure they have said what they mean. The attitude to *Harmonium* which they more or less share is not that different from Wilson's, and in some respects it is worse. Wilson at least admitted the possibility of a limited interest in the "purely verbal" poetry. It is silly to praise the idea of the "supreme fiction" and simultaneously have a sort of violent revulsion from the only form it can take, the only form in which it had any interest for Stevens. These critics' attention to the later poems has not enabled them to notice better what Stevens achieved in the earlier books. (It is fair to add, though, that all of these critics do better when they are paying attention to individual poems, including poems in *Harmonium*. It is possible to miss this in the murk of Bloom's prose, but he knows minutely the most obscure references, the subtlest puns in the poems, showing an awesome line-by-line knowledge of Stevens' work. But the theory is all about something else.)

Winters, who did not like the language of *The Comedian* either, had very different reasons and deserves to be considered separately.

What I wish the reader to note is this: that the passage describes Crispin's taking leave of his art [see my remarks on this passage in chapter 2] and describes also his refusal to use his art in the process of leave-taking, because the art is, after all, futile and contemptible. Yet for Stevens himself the entire poem is a kind of tentative leave-taking; he has not the courage to act as his hero does and be done with it, so he practices the art which he cannot justify and describes it in terms of contempt.

Furthermore, the chief instrument of irony in this passage, and throughout the poem, and indeed throughout much of the rest of Stevens, is a curious variant on the self-ridicule, the romantic irony, with which we are familiar from Byron through Laforgue and his modern disciples; the instrument is self-parody, a parody occasionally subtle, often clumsy, of the refined and immutable style of Stevens at his best. (Winters, 243)

Winters seems to have taken such a powerful dislike to the style of *The Comedian* that he did not have the patience to grasp the way Stevens' arguments justify the style. Unlike Vendler and Pearce, he didn't object to the poem's being poetry. Winters also thought that Stevens' philosophy, as far as he understood it, was untenable and was actually causing the deterioration of Stevens' art. (He relented in this judgment somewhat; in the postscript to "The Hedonist's Progress" he said that Stevens' talent had not decayed as much as he had anticipated it would [Winters, 459].) Winters knew, nevertheless, that *Harmonium* represented original thinking from the outset.

Aside from the work of Winters, Cunningham, and a few others, it would appear that the older, conventional view of Stevens as the aesthete / hedonist has been overlaid by a new conventional attitude, Stevens the prophet and theorist of literature. On the one hand, he's literary history's plaything: on the other, he may almost be an English Professor.

Chapter Five

An observer taking a bird's-eye-view of painting, sculpture, dance, theater, music, poetry, fiction, and architecture in Europe (Russia included) and the United States might admit that modernism seemed to be a single process of change taking place roughly in about the first thirty years of this century (Baudelaire, Corbière, Rimbaud, Mallarmé being the precursors of this movement in poetry). That is probably a generous estimate, including some of the time when the new had been well-established in some places (Paris, New York) and was making its way to others (Michigan? Mexico?). In some places (the Amazon rain forest) nothing happened. And in others, when modernist art finally arrived, it did not necessarily make a big difference in how people lived their lives. In every place that modernist innovation reached, it met something that was already there and was itself modified by that something. It did not escape having a certain amount of the fantastically fortuitous: how could any laws of cultural development explain the physical capacity, the beauty and temperament of Vaçlav Nijinsky? Why should Pound—who was such an influential leader of the movement in poetry in English, who wrote such variously effective poems and supported the work of almost all the great names in twentieth-century literature of the period—have so soon been overcome by the obsession that entangled him with the fascists? (These last, of course, were modern too.) And why should he have continued to produce the *Cantos*? We can't make out these complications and details from a bird's-eye-view. The form of the *Cantos* owes something to the circumstances of Pound's life, which were not like the circumstances of any other person's. Maybe the *Cantos* aren't all readable, and maybe they show a lack of sustained concentration on a subject for its own sake outside of Pound's general urge to write them. The effects of his obsession, physical and mental, external and internal, show in the poems. At the same time he was led into his obsessions by, among other things, ideas about art that produced humane, intelligent poems. Pound wrote his poems, but his whole life is one of the tragic instances of how poetry is bound up with history and with the material circumstances of the individual's life and temperament, in ways that are contradictory, so that we cannot be fair to history or to Pound without carefully discriminating among all those variables. And yet insofar as we are all living in a sadder and uglier world because of that war whose instigators were supported by people Pound didn't have the judgment not to be taken in by, we live unable to close the book on that war and on Pound for his part in it. So much that happens in the real world is inconclusive because nothing really ends. Except one wonders, too, how much meaningful support could have been given by the tedious, incoherent ravings in his radio broadcasts that would have bored and puzzled even a fascist.

Stevens is one of the important modernist poets. In his work we find formal innovation, new subject matter, and the feeling that something separates him from the past. These features of his work can also be found to some degree in any of the writers considered modern; Joyce, Hemingway, and Lawrence have these features in their work also. All of these people were idiosyncratic, difficult; they were not like anybody else and they were not like each other.

The Comedian as the Letter C tells the story of Crispin's questioning of poetic tradition and of his attempts to write a true, authentic poetry. Crispin tries and rejects various formulas and attitudes and ends his journeyings in uncertainty about his future in poetry. Crispin at the end of the poem knows two things: he knows that he does not *know* what the truth is in poetry, and he knows that the truth is what he wants, needs to write. In another chapter I have suggested that Stevens' need to write the truth is like Wordsworth's, and results in his disdain for "the common inheritance of poets" (Wordsworth, 323). Stevens expresses his dissatisfaction with the poetic conventions that are his inheritance in the way he uses language. *The Comedian as the Letter C* tells of Crispin's perceiving

> That coolness for his heat came suddenly,
> And only, in the fables that he scrawled,
> With his own quill, in its indigenous dew, (CP, 31)

and in his having the recourse of deliberately flouting the rules of poetry that dictated the state of the art. He reminds himself of his need for his own voice in section IV:

> What was the purpose of his pilgrimage,
> Whatever shape it took in Crispin's mind,
> If not, when all is said, to drive away
> The shadows of his fellows from the skies,
> And, from their stale intelligence released,
> To make a new intelligence prevail? (CP, 37)

This need for an individual idiom is the motive for the style of Stevens' "first, central hymns" (CP, 37), those poems in which we see the evidence of great poetic power, but also see "The appointed power unwielded from disdain" (CP, 37). I have mentioned, in the chapter on *The Comedian*, Stevens' use of goofy noises. J.V. Cunningham describes a few more of Stevens' strategies.

> The first thing that strikes the reader of Wallace Stevens, and the quality for which he was for a long time best known, is the piquant, brilliant, and odd surface of his poems. They are full of nonsense cries, full of virtuoso lines . . . which unexpectedly make grammar and sense if you read them slowly with closed ears. They are thronged with exotic place-names, but not the customary ones of late romantic poetry; instead of "Quinquereme of Nineveh from distant Ophir" there is "a woman of Lhassa," there is Yucatan. Rare birds fly, "the green toucan," and tropical fruits abound, especially the pineapple. Odd characters appear—Crispin, Redwood Roamer, Badroulbadour, black Sly, Nanzia Nunzio—and are addressed in various languages—my semblables, Nino, ephebi, o iuventes, of filii. And they wear strange hats. (Cunningham, 228)

It's as if Stevens had invented his own fictional, private, poetic tradition, like the real one, having birds, flowers, people, places, some of which also were in the other tradition. Like the real tradition, it has an unorganized body of knowledge (mythological personages or historical ones), its tones of voice, its choice words and recurring motifs, its own metaphors and rules of decorum.

Stevens also invents new voices, for example in "Hibiscus on the Sleeping Shores," a poem that invites comparison with Keats' "On First Looking Into Chapman's Homer" or "On Seeing the Elgin Marbles," or, most interestingly, with Wordsworth's "I Wandered Lonely as a Cloud."

> I say now, Fernando, that on that day
> The mind roams as a moth roams,
> Among the blooms beyond the open sand;

And that whatever noise the motion of the waves
Made on the sea-weeds and the covered stones
Disturbed not even the most idle ear.

Then it was that that monstered moth
Which had lain folded against the blue
And the colored purple of the lazy sea,

And which had drowsed along the bony shores
Shut to the blather that the water made,
Rose up besprent and sought the flaming red

Dabbled with yellow pollen—red as red
As the flag above the old cafe
And roamed there all the stupid afternoon.
(*CP*, 22–23)

    The poem has a perfectly respectable subject, a peculiar state of attention to a single object. (Remember Keats' "My heart sinks and a drowsy numbness pains / My sense. . . . ") The correspondence with the familiar poem by Wordsworth is even more striking. Compare Wordsworth's

> I wandered lonely as a cloud
> That floats on high o'er vales and hills,

to Stevens'

> I say now, Fernando, that on that day
> The mind roams as a moth roams,
> Among the blooms beyond the open sand;

Wordsworth's

> When all at once I saw a crowd,
> A host, of golden daffodils;

to Stevens' "monstered moth," which

> Rose up besprent and sought the flaming red
> Dabbled with yellow pollen—red as red
> As the flag above the old cafe—

Wordsworth's

> I gazed—and gazed—but little thought
> What wealth to me the show had brought

while Stevens' moth "roamed there all the stupid afternoon."

A few phrases establish the poem's tone of voice: "I say, now, Fernando"—the pedestrian, first-name informality; can one say anything very ponderous beginning "I say now"?—the sea's "bony shores," the water's "blather," "the stupid afternoon." Such phrases are the language of a person who either does not know or does not care to put his experience in the terms or with the feelings which romanticism has provided for that experience. An individual's attention is caught up by a flower: except that on this particular occasion the attention has that maddening clumsy, repetitive imprecision that the movements of moths have. The color of the flower itself is compared—unthinkable in romantic poetry, late or early—to "the flag above the old cafe." Because to compare a flower to anything pertaining to a commercial enterprise is to demote it. The sea here, as almost always in Stevens' poems, appears in its character of unceasing garrulousness.

Even as we recognize the romantic subject (the flower) we also see how it can be spoken of in a poem in an unromantic voice and still be there as an experience. "Hibiscus on the Sleeping Shores" is a poem about language, but it is still a poem about a flower and about the mind.

In the way the language works, "Hibiscus" is similar to "The Ordinary Women" (CP, 10), which tells a story: the passage of the ordinary women from poverty to opulence to disillusionment.

Again, the subject and setting, and even details of the furniture and dress, are the sorts of things that, according to the romantic, one expects in poems. But there is something strangely artificial too; the poem is opaque. "The Ordinary Women" seems to resist attempts to locate Stevens in it. The story is disembodied, an utterly frivolous fiction, to which Winters' observation on Poe might apply: "If, indeed, certain human experiences are admitted as legitimate subjects, they are admitted . . . because the poet cannot write without writing about something . . ." (Winters, 243).

But Stevens is thinking in the poem's diction, where the rhymes seem to be aspiring to the dignity and drama of Keats, or of *The Rime of the Ancient Mariner*,[1] but somehow never manage it. They sound as though they should, but they don't:

> catarrhs / guitars
> turned from their want / and, nonchalant
> vapid haze / window bays
> The diamond point / the sapphire point

These rhymes are not nonsensical; each phrase quoted here contributes, literally, to the story that is being told. If "The Ordinary Women" is a bit of "pure poetry" that exists as an object to be appreciated, that appreciating is undermined by the deliberate improprieties of the language. Like the rhymes are the excesses of alliteration: "lacquered loges," "canting curlicues," and "gaunt guitarists." The poem reveals the reliance of poetry on some notion of decorum. Or perhaps poetry's independence of it.

Stevens wrote about "Cortège for Rosenbloom" (*CP*, 79):

From time immemorial the philosophers and others have daubed the sky with dazzle paint. But it all comes down to the proverbial six feet of earth in the end. This is true of Rosenbloom as of Alcibiades. It cannot be possible that they have never munched

this chestnut at Tufts. The ceremonies are amusing. Why not fill
the sky with scaffolds and stairs, and go about like genuine realists?
(*L*, 223)

The thought echoes the sixth stanza of *Sunday Morning*:

> Alas, that they should wear our colors there,
> The silken weavings of our afternoons,
> And pick the strings of our insipid lutes!

though the tone of "Cortège for Rosenbloom" is deadpan to the
earnestness here. The heaven that *Sunday Morning* criticizes in
these lines is the philosophers' and scene painters' dazzle-painted
one. The heaven of "Cortège for Rosenbloom" is imagined by a
person with a steadier (even if only slightly steadier) sense of
reality. This person is a realist because his inventions are drawn
from that reality, not from conventions, that had their origins in
earlier versions of reality, of what heaven should look like. Our
understanding of what is imagined in the poem comes from the
sound of the poem, from repetition in the first stanza of the same
heavy words to the weird, tinny festiveness of the next two to the
last. These sounds mimic the noises to be heard in that heaven,
from the "tread, on a hundred legs" of Rosenbloom's "finical
carriers," through galumphing repetitions of "tread" and "dead,"
to the fantastic last three stanzas. The peculiar sound that
eventually takes over is also something imagined about heaven.

> To a chirr of gongs
> And a chitter of cries
> And the heavy thrum
> Of the endless tread
> That they tread;
>
> To a jangle of doom
> And a jumble of words
> Of the intense poem
> Of the strictest prose
> Of Rosenbloom. (*CP*, 80)

Cortege for Rosenbloom carries out an intention expressed in "The Plot Against The Giant."

> *First Girl*
> When this yokel comes maundering,
> Whetting his hacker,
> I shall run before him,
> Diffusing the civilest odors
> Out of geraniums and unsmelled flowers.
> It will check him.
> *Second Girl*
> I shall run before him,
> Arching cloths besprinkled with colors
> As small as fish-eggs.
> The threads
> Will abash him.
> *Third Girl*
> Oh, la . . . le pauvre!
> I shall run before him,
> With a curious puffing.
> He will bend his ear then.
> I shall whisper
> Heavenly labials in a world of gutturals.
> It will undo him. (CP, 6–7)

Instead of the harmoniousness of, say, Keats' "Forlorn! the very word is like a bell / To toll me back from thee to my sole self!"— the sort of thing people mean when they speak of the romantic— we can expect very different kinds of word-music.

It isn't only in the studied indecorousness of his diction that Stevens makes his comments. "Of Heaven Considered as a Tomb" uses a really elegant, grand style to present a curious vignette of the dead, "the darkened ghosts of our old comedy."

> Do they believe they range the gusty cold,
> With lanterns borne aloft to light the way,

> Freemen of death, about and still about
> To find whatever it is they seek? Or does
> That burial, pillared up each day as port
> And spiritous passage into nothingness,
> Foretell each night the one abysmal night,
> When the host shall no more wander, nor the light
> Of the steadfast lanterns creep across the dark?
> Make hue among the dark comedians,
> Halloo them in the topmost distances
> For answer from their icy Elysée. (CP, 56)

Like Wordsworth, Stevens is using the grand style for his own purposes, and just as Wordsworth took it from Milton for un-Miltonic purposes, the scene that Stevens describes here would probably have caused Wordsworth to think he was using the style for unpoetic, self-parodic motives.

Stevens uses an exalted style in "Invective Against Swans" to describe a frame of mind that is far from exalted:

> The soul, O ganders, flies beyond the parks
> And far beyond the discords of the wind.
>
> A bronze rain from the sun descending marks
> The death of summer, which that time endures
>
> Like one who scrawls a listless testament
> Of golden quirks and Paphian caricatures,
>
> Bequeathing your white feathers to the moon
> And giving your bland motions to the air.
>
> Behold, already on the long parades
> The crows anoint the statues with their dirt.
>
> And the soul, O ganders, being lonely, flies
> Beyond your chilly chariots, to the skies. (CP,4)

It is from the title that we are to understand that the language of the poem is the invective, i.e., what we call invective: verbal abuse.

Harmonium has the most lively poetic effects, the greatest variety of voices. In *The Comedian as the Letter C* and *Le Monocle de Mon Oncle* the novelty and variety of language are sustained at some length. Every poem, almost, shows a new invention; the great virtue of *Harmonium* is what is most apparent and most puzzling to the newcomer to Stevens: the *absence* of what Helen Vendler called "a restricted set of formal counters adequate to feeling and knowledge" (Vendler, 1984, 5). Attentive reading of Stevens' poems would make a reader tend to question all the values that are implied in such a definition of a poet's mature style. Stevens has his own ideas about style, and a description of his style has to in some way take account of those ideas. Why "restricted?" How do we know it was a set? What are "formal counters?" By what criteria were these formal counters judged to be appropriate? Vendler's terms, though she evidently intends that they be neutral, imply without identifying what she seems to believe are unquestionable, universally recognized aesthetic values. Restricted ones, at that. In *Harmonium* the unrestricted variety of styles, the skepticism regarding the whole notion of appropriateness, the wealth of word-music effects as profuse and chaotic and even at times as haphazard as Crispin's Yucatan jungle, all call into question and deliberately exceed the values by which Vendler is judging Stevens' work.

The judgment exercised by the reader is like a tactful awareness of the poet's intelligence, as opposed to a mere listening out for mannerisms. The syntax and the words are very important— essential, since they are all we have on the page. The poem's potential to interest me comes from the sense I have, at first, of liveliness. I might not get all of it at once, I can enjoy parts I am not sure I understand, because I am aware of the intelligence that might tell me something new, or whose presence, within the form of the poem, is interesting. That presence is most real as something experienced. An explanation is like a theory: even a good theory is vulnerable for the reason Stevens gives against explanations.[2]

"The Curtains in the House of the Metaphysician" (*CP*, 62) has another obvious Wordsworth theme, that of "A Night-Piece" (Wordsworth, 190) but the tone of "The Curtains" is very different from that of "A Night-Piece" and different also from "Hibiscus."

> It comes about that the drifting of these curtains
> Is full of long motions; as the ponderous
> Deflations of distance; or as clouds
> Inseparable from their afternoons;
> Or the changing of light, the dropping
> Of the silence, wide sleep and solitude
> Of night, in which all motion
> Is beyond us, as the firmament,
> Up-rising and down-falling, bares
> The last largeness, bold to see. (*CP*, 62)

It might be noted also that one conspicuous feature of Wordsworth's poems is their optimistic ecstasy. Wordsworth speaks confidently of "that inward eye which is the bliss of solitude" (Wordsworth, 293); and the traveller who sees the clouds part, is exalted and strengthened somehow by the vision of the moon and infinite space. The changes of mood in both Wordsworth's poems occur instantaneously. The protagonist sheds his brooding and uncertainty. In Stevens' poems, even with their different voices, some uncertainty remains. The "last largeness" is put at a great distance from the person who sees it. The "last largeness" is bareness and solitude, as well as grandeur. Neither it nor the hibiscus appear to their observers as a source of comfort. What connects Stevens' two poems is a metaphysical loneliness, implied only in the absence of ecstacy from the language of the poems: like a scrupulously kept secret. One reason why we can infer that loneliness here is because it is to be found in so many other poems, *Sunday Morning* most importantly, where it is treated more directly. This loneliness has nothing to do with romanticism, except insofar as romanticism was for a brief time able to give the consolation for that specific loneliness or separatedness that belief in religion used to give. "Palace of the Babies" talks about the loneliness of unbelief.

> The walker in the moonlight walked alone,
> And each blank window of the building balked
> His loneliness and what was in his mind:
>
> If in a shimmering room the babies came,
> Drawn close by dreams of fledgling wing,
> It was because night nursed them in its fold.
>
> Night nursed not him in whose dark mind
> The clambering wings of birds of black revolved,
> Making harsh torment of the solitude.
>
> The walker in the moonlight walked alone,
> And in his heart his disbelief lay cold.
> His broad-brimmed hat came close upon his eyes.
> (*CP*, 77)

As we have seen in *Sunday Morning*, the person who does not believe has to manage without belief. For Stevens, this means also managing his longing for something to believe. In "The Emperor of Ice-Cream" it is easy to resist the desire for belief:

> Call the roller of big cigars,
> The muscular one, and bid him whip
> In kitchen cups concupiscent curds.
> Let the wenches dawdle in such dress
> As they are used to wear, and let the boys
> Bring flowers in last month's newspapers.
> Let be be finale of seem.
> The only emperor is the emperor of ice-cream.

> Take from the dresser of deal,
> Lacking the three glass knobs, that sheet
> On which she embroidered fantails once
> And spread it so as to cover her face.
> If her horny feet protrude, they come
> To show how cold she is, and dumb.
> Let the lamp affix its beam.
> The only emperor is the emperor of ice-cream.
> (CP, 64)

Here is an interesting experiment anyone can try if he or she has followed me this far: first, find an intelligent and discerning person who is perhaps not very interested in or familiar with Stevens' poems; this is not as difficult as it might seem. Get this person to read "The Emperor of Ice-Cream." (This person, obviously, has to be honest and not trying to ingratiate himself with you, i.e. willing to say "I don't get it.") Then try to explain, using only the one poem, why it is about belief. What details of that scene have anything to do with belief? "The Emperor of Ice-Cream" is frequently anthologized, and yet, standing by itself it reads like lively wordplay that has carefully crafted the illusion of referring to something. We start out hearing some of the objects as symbols. But what could a deal dresser missing a few glass knobs be a symbol of? And a dead woman's protruding feet are much too distracting as objects in themselves to be pointing to something transcendent. The poem does refer to something, of course. The line "let be be finale of seem" can be explained. But it is not a simple task to explain what it has to do with the action in the rest of the poem. Part of the meaning of the poem comes from the speaker's zest for details, which he possesses even in this setting. The attitude is expressed in the tone of voice and in details such as the fantails embroidered on the sheet. Why notice the embroidery now? These little, illuminated details nevertheless come to the narrator's attention in the flow of the practical tasks. It's the bright, unillusioned sufficiency of all this together that makes the narrator say "Let be be finale of seem." All of which can be explained to someone, but doesn't guarantee that they will see it for themselves. This experiment reveals two things: (1) how Stevens' poems are interrelated, and (2) how even though they are interrelated the individual poem makes a very vigorous claim—it demands that we learn to think in its idiom.

This list of instructions tells us no more and no less about the world than does the last stanza of *Sunday Morning:*

> We live in an old chaos of the sun,
> Or old dependency of day and night,
> Or island solitude, unsponsored, free,
> Of that wide water, inescapable.
> Deer walk upon our mountains, and the quail
> Whistle about us their spontaneous cries;
> Sweet berries ripen in the wilderness;
> And, in the isolation of the sky,
> At evening, casual flocks of pigeons make
> Ambiguous undulations as they sink,
> Downward to darkness, on extended wings. (CP, 70)

And it does not tell us more or less about the world than does "The Snow Man," which is about the difficulty of resisting the desire to believe.

> One must have a mind of winter
> To regard the frost and the boughs
> Of the pine-trees crusted with snow;
>
> And have been cold a long time
> To behold the junipers shagged with ice,
> The spruces rough in the distant glitter
>
> Of the January sun; and not to think
> Of any misery in the sound of the wind,
> In the sound of a few leaves. . . . (CP, 9–10)

The listener, who beholds "nothing that is not there and the nothing that is," is for a moment able to regard, that is, to look attentively at the landscape and to see it purified of emotional associations fostered by his deluding imagination. But Stevens uses a harsh word for the landscape so purified: he calls it "nothing." He could just as logically have called it "everything." The bitterness in the last line suggests doubt at the value of having achieved this state of vision. The doubt arises because of the effort it takes ("One must have a mind of winter . . . / And have been cold a very long time") to subdue the listener's imagination.

> Sometimes I wish I wore no crown—that I trod on something thicker than air—that there were no robins, or peach dumplings, or violets in my world—that I was the proprietor of a patent medicine store—or manufactured pants for the trade—and that my name was Asa Snuff. But alas! the tormenting harmonies sweep around my hat, my bosom swells with "agonies and exultations"—and I pose. (L, 48)

We saw a similar effort made in "Study of Two Pears." In chapter 3 I mentioned Ezra Pound's program for the reform of poetry and culture. I said that Stevens had no ambitions of that kind. Even though nobody sensible endorses Pound's reforming ambitions, Stevens has been criticized for not having any. This difference was a difference in temperaments. But we can at this point begin to see that Stevens was haunted by questions that neither Pound nor any of the other respectable modernist reformers gave themselves too much trouble about. These questions took hold of Stevens and did not take hold of them. Stevens' formal innovations addressed a problem of his imagination and temperament that is outlined in the journal entry above, thirteen years before any of the modern poems were written.

The vision he attains in "The Snow Man" is another solution, though not a completely satisfactory one, first of all because of the vitality of his imagination: perhaps no poem suggests its variousness and energy better than *The Comedian*. Crispin's appetite for truth is bedevilled by the way his imagination seizes and is fired by ideas. For instance, his "native aesthetic" idea. Or when, in Yucatan

> . . . this odd
> Discoverer walked through the harbor streets
> Inspecting the cabildo, the facade
> Of the cathedral, making notes . . . (*CP*, 32)

he is confidently acting in accordance with one idea of the place as the storm approaches that will change that very idea. Or at sea when he catches a glimpse of himself—"A skinny sailor," "this short-shanks" (*CP*, 28). Stevens makes a direct statement of the vitality of imagination in "Saint John and the Back-Ache":

> The mind is the terriblest force in the world, father,
> Because, in chief, it, only, can defend
> Against itself. (*CP*, 436)

There is just the difficulty of subduing the imagination: "The pears are not seen / As the observer wills," says the observer in "Study of Two Pears" (*CP*, 196), as he makes an effort of will and of imagination to look at the pears and see their essential "pearness," resisting the immediate impulse to describe them as compared with something else. Are pears really "yellow forms / Composed of curves / Bulging toward the base?" Is this a definition of a pear? Of course it isn't. Stevens is trying not to be distracted by similes, or transformations of pears into other things in his mind. He is concentrating, with effort, only on the properties of the pears: shape, proportion, color, the way they fit in space, surface details, the way they reflect light and cast a shadow. These are their properties *as seen*, that distinguish them from walnuts, nails, mice, *as seen*. Stevens also wants to distinguish between what belongs to the pears and what his own imagination has brought to them.

In 1941, C.L. Daughtry, a co-worker of Stevens' at the

Hartford, sent him some persimmons. In the note he sent thanking Daughtry for the fruit, Stevens wrote,

> . . . [W]ild persimmons make one feel like a hungry man in the woods. As I ate them, I thought of opossums and birds, and the antique Japanese prints in black and white, in which monkeys are eating persimmons in bare trees. There is nothing more desolate than a persimmon tree with the old ripe fruit hanging on it. . . . (L, 394)

Are these persimmons seen as the observer wills? Obviously the recollections that came to Stevens are not what we might call "properties" of persimmons.

Strictly speaking, of course, we can't talk about "properties" of persimmons or pears: we might use the terms when talking about cooking, or just metaphorically. The distinction that the old philosophers were trying to make, we now know, simply does not describe the phenomenon except in a provisional way. A physicist might say there are properties of matter / energy that make persimmons in general or those four on the table possible. It seems just as accurate to say that a persimmon is a stage or an episode as that it has properties. These are both metaphorical descriptions, saying something about the persimmon but not saying everything. A botanist and a physicist would not have any professional interest in what interests Stevens about the persimmons. But they might as humans, who inhabit a universe that includes persimmons. It happens that their work concentrates on some things to do with persimmons and not on others. This limitation is a practical necessity, not an ideological dictate.

Common knowledge can include what the scientists know; it includes the properties of pears, it includes the concept that there are properties of pears, which has in this forum to compete against the idea that pears do not have properties. It includes recollections evoked by persimmons. It depends heavily on metaphor which allows you to speak of an object selectively. It has economy—what if every time you referred to a dog you had to state it in terms of everything that was known about dogs?—and in the necessity for that economy is implicit the pressure of time and the reality of living creatures' needs and purposes. It is not a dogma or theory, does not possess or need structural self-consistency, so its inconsistency and self-contradictoriness need not be explained by a "principle of inherent contradiction in all utterance" or by the death of God. It is an activity.[3]

The Comedian does not have a theory of poetry. Crispin starts out with something he thinks he knows: a seemingly self-evident, well-established, authoritative idea. He wants to write the truth: he has curiosity and intellectual honesty, and the first thing he discovers is that the truth is not all that obvious. Crispin's search involves an investigation into poetic convention: this is because poetry is Crispin's medium. His adventures, though, are not just an episode in literary history. Because common knowledge, common speech, is poetic. When Stevens says that Crispin "lives in a poetic atmosphere, as we all do," he doesn't mean that we need to take time to appreciate "the things that really matter." Nor does he mean to be overvaluing our high cultural inheritance or its influence. He means that the way we think, what we call our understanding, is a poetic faculty. Stevens called "The Emperor of Ice-Cream" "a good example of a poem that has its own singularity." Explaining himself, he continues:

> But after all, the point of that poem is not its meaning. When people think of poems as integrations, they are thinking usually of integration of ideas; that is to say, of what they mean. However, a poem must have a peculiarity, as if it was the momentarily complete idiom of that which prompts it, even if that which prompts it is the vaguest emotion. This character seems to be one of the consequences of concentration. (L, 500)

When we need to understand or "integrate" our experience, we reach towards it with all our faculties. We are trying to take in as much of it as possible, with our whole selves. And we want to remember it, as much of it as we can. Concentration is important because it is prolonged, exclusive attention to a particular object. In the mind, as in the poem, we are interested primarily in, to use Stevens' words, "not ideas about the thing but the thing itself." It's true that we impose form, we're selective in memory. But the order and selectivity have to take account of the greatest range of complexity and detail; the difficulty is that these are always slipping away.

That the action of attention and memory is like the act of writing a poem—as Stevens describes it here—is one of the most persistent and compelling arguments in all of Stevens' work. There is more than one poem dealing with it in each book. In *Harmonium*, it is the subject of "On the Manner of Addressing Clouds."

> Gloomy grammarians in golden gowns,
> Meekly you keep the mortal rendezvous,
> Eliciting the still sustaining pomps
> Of speech which are like music so profound
> They seem an exaltation without sound.
> Funest philosophers and ponderers,
> Their evocations are the speech of clouds.
> So speech of your professionals returns
> In the casual evocations of your tread
> Across the stale, mysterious seasons. These
> Are the music of meet resignation; these
> The responsive, still sustaining pomps for you
> To magnify, if in that drifting waste
> You are to be accompanied by more
> Than mute bare splendors of the sun and moon. (CP, 55)

That the poetry of an object, our fictions about it, may be an indispensable part of the way we know it, occurs to Crispin. On his river voyage he recognizes that the imagination filters what he sees because he gets what he believes is a glimpse of reality undistorted by previous ideas. He also just happens to be out of ideas at the time. But later another possibility emerges.

Whoever hunts a matinal continent
May, after all, stop short before a plum
And be content and still be realist.
The words of things entangle and confuse.
The plum survives its poems. It may hang
In the sunshine placidly, colored by ground
Obliquities of those who pass beneath,
Harlequined and mazily dewed and mauved
In bloom. Yet it survives in its own form,
Beyond these changes, good, fat, guzzly fruit. (CP, 41)

The plum is "harlequined and mazily dewed and mauved" by
the imaginations of those who pass underneath it, rather like the
way the persimmons live in Stevens' imagination in his letter to
Daughtry. In "The Sense of the Sleight-of-Hand Man" the
imagination's products and the moment-by-moment marvels of
ordinary life peacefully co-exist.

Could you have said the bluejay suddenly
Would swoop to earth? It is a wheel, the rays
Around the sun. The wheel survives the myths.
The fire eye in the clouds survives the gods.
To think of a dove with an eye of grenadine
And pines that are cornets, so it occurs,
And a little island full of geese and stars . . . (CP, 222)

Myths of the sun, the dove, the pines that are cornets, are
instances of what the imagination can make out of its isolated
activity or from an encounter with the object. Here, the imagined
is part of knowledge. "The Glass of Water," like the Florida
poems of *Harmonium*, shows how imaginary forms can reveal
something true about experience.

That the glass would melt in heat,
That the water would freeze in cold,
Shows that this object is merely a state,

One of many, between two poles. So,
In the metaphysical, there are these poles.

Here in the center stands the glass. Light
Is the lion that comes down to drink. There
And in that state, the glass is a pool.
Ruddy are his eyes and ruddy are his claws
When light comes down to wet his frothy jaws.

And in the water winding weeds move round. (CP,
197)

As the glass of water is present in one of a number of possible
physical states, so is it present to the mind in one of a number of
possible metaphysical (or metaphorical) states. We can see many
different things when we regard a glass of water. A simple object
lives a complicated life in our minds, and what is true for the
glass is true for "the center of our lives, this time, this day" (CP,
198). The metaphor "Light is the lion that comes down to drink"
does not just cleverly describe an ordinary object: it also reveals
something about our knowledge of objects. The line would have
another meaning if Stevens had written "Light is *like* the lion
that comes down to drink." The metaphor is not only an
expression of similarity, because it is an expression of the way the
object is being experienced.

When we judge the progress and conclusion of Crispin's
adventures, we ought to consider the indestructibility and persist-
ence of metaphors as the idiom of experience. The children in
"A Postcard from the Volcano" (CP, 158) are not conscious of
the life of the past, the history of their own speech and knowledge: because they are children. In "Questions are Remarks,"
Stevens makes the same point about another child.

His question is complete because it contains
His utmost statement. It is his own array,
His own pageant and procession and display. . . . (CP, 462)

2>3

Children don't know that what they see and how they see are an inheritance, not of Donne or Jane Austen or Freud, but of casual forms of speech, of metaphors, of fragments of myth, that persist after the original, intense experience has faded from memory.

> Children picking up our bones
> Will never know that these were once
> As quick as foxes on the hill;
> . . .
> And least will guess that with our bones
> We left much more, left what still is
> The look of things, left what we felt
>
> At what we saw. . . . (CP, 158–159)

The reason as we saw it articulated in "On the Manner of Addressing Clouds" is that our speech informs their perception.

> We knew for long the mansion's look
> And what we said of it became
>
> A part of what it is. . . . (CP. 159)

In these poems it seems acceptable to Stevens that objects of experience live for us in our speech and our common knowledge. In others the poverty and staleness of that knowledge disgusts or frustrates him. "Delightful Evening" is about an evening which is delightful in spite of "The twilight overfull / Of wormy metaphors" (CP, 162). A period of inability to have an experience unmediated by "wormy metaphors" is described in "Cuisine Bourgeoise" as "These days of disinheritance," and compared to

> . . . the season when, after summer,
> It is summer and it is not, it is autumn
> And it is not, it is day and it is not,
> As if last night's lamps continued to burn,
> As if yesterday's people continued to watch

The sky, half porcelain, preferring that
To shaking out heavy bodies in the glares
Of this present, this science, this unrecognized,
This outpost, this douce, this dumb, this dead, in which
We feast on human heads . . . (CP, 227)

Stevens wrote to Hi Simons: "Powerful integrations of the imagination are difficult to get away from. I am surprised that you
have any difficulty with this, when the chances are that every day
you see all sorts of things through the eyes of other people in
terms of their imaginations" (L, 403).

The time of year, it is worth noting here, is another version
of the season of "Banal Sojourn."

Moisture and heat have swollen the garden into a slum of
    bloom
Pardie! Summer is like a fat beast, sleepy in mildew,
Our old bane, green and bloated, serene, who cries,
"That bliss of stars, that princox of evening heaven!"
    reminding of seasons,
When radiance came running down, slim through the
    bareness. (CP, 62–63)

The people in "Cuisine Bourgeoise" feast on human heads
because they are caught in a similar slack time, with stale
thoughts that, like the thoughts in sleep of "Anecdote of Canna"
(CP, 55), meet only themselves. Because in "Anecdote of
Canna" this separation from the real is natural and temporary, it
is not associated with anguish, the bitterness, of poems like "The
Man Whose Pharynx was Bad":

The time of year has grown indifferent.
Mildew of summer and the deepening snow
Are both alike in the routine I know.
I am too dumbly in my being pent.
    . . .

The malady of the quotidian . . .
Perhaps, if winter once could penetrate
Through all its purples to the final slate,
Persisting bleakly in an icy haze,

One might in turn become less diffident,
Out of such mildew plucking neater mould
And spouting new orations of the cold.
One might. One might. But time will not relent. (CP, 96)

For the character X in "Anecdote of Canna," also, ". . . thought that wakes / In sleep may never meet another thought / Or thing. . . ." (CP, 55). Stevens explained these lines in a letter to Hi Simons:

> . . . [T]hought that wakes in sleep differs from waking thought because thought in sleep "may never meet another thought or thing," *for the reason that it meets only itself.* [Stevens' emphasis] It has not the benefit of the external. When the sleeper wakes reality has the dewiness that reality should have as reality. (L, 465)

In "Cuisine Bourgeoise" and "Banal Sojourn" the state of mind is like that of X in his dream, if X were unable to wake up to the dewiness of reality. In these two we know that the speaker is awake. His separation from reality, its failure to refresh his imagination, imposes the poverty of dreams on his waking experience.

When X observes the canna and then continues to observe, it is because of the canna's separate existence from his own ideas. "His eye clings to reality and sates itself in it or on it" (L, 465). For the person with the eye that clings to reality, a number of possibilities may develop. One occurs in "The Emperor of Ice-Cream," where reality is engrossing even in its most commonplace and dingy details, the opposite of the overblown irrelevance of "Banal Sojourn." The second occurs when the observer finds reality unmixed with imagination to be a little too bare. In "The Snow Man" and "Palace of the Babies" the disbeliever tries to subdue his longing to believe. The third possibility is that the observer can indulge his "blessed rage for order" (CP, 130) instead of trying to get rid of it. This last sets him on some adventures: the quest for new "sovereign images," in the localism of "Anecdote of Men by the Thousand"; in the Florida poems and the Yucatan scenes of *The Comedian* the landscape itself invites the observer to imagine order, an intelligence that has fashioned its peculiar beauty.

The "exhilaration of reality," then, is like the experience of the woman in *Sunday Morning*. It is the predicament described in "'To the One of Fictive Music,'"[4] that begins with the advice to the muse that

> . . . no thread
> Of cloudy silver sprinkles in your gown
> Its venom of renown, and on your head
> No crown is simpler than the simple hair. (CP. 87)

Her music, which is "summoned by the birth / That separates us from the wind and sea, / Yet leaves us in them" is most expressive of human life when it most faithfully describes the world.

> . . . of all vigils musing the obscure,
> That apprehends the most which sees and names,
> As in your name, an image that is sure,
> Among the arrant spices of the sun,
> O bough and bush and scented vine, in whom
> We give ourselves our likest issuance. (CP, 88)

But the imagination's fictions, untrue as they are, may be a kind of consolation for our loneliness in being separated from the earth. "Likeness" may not be enough.

> Yet not too like, yet not so like to be
> Too near, too clear, saving a little to endow
> Our feigning with the strange unlike, whence springs

The difference that heavenly pity brings.
For this, musician, in your girdle fixed
Bear other perfumes. On your pale head wear
A band entwining, set with fatal stones.
Unreal, give back to us what once you gave:
The imagination that we spurned and crave. (CP, 88)

This predicament is also the theme of "Anatomy of Monotony."
It persists through all the books of the *Collected Poems*. In "No
Possum, No Sop, No Taters" it is possible to see the most bracing
benefits of the external:

It is in this solitude, a syllable,
Out of these gawky flitterings,

Intones its single emptiness,
The savagest hollow of winter-sound.

It is here, in this bad, that we reach
The last purity of the knowledge of good.

The crow looks rusty as he rises up,
Bright is the malice in his eye . . .

One joins him there for company,
But at a distance, in another tree. (CP, 293)

In "The Plain Sense of Things" this solitude and bleakness are
needed.

. . . the absence of the imagination had
Itself to be imagined. The great pond,
The plain sense of it, without reflections, leaves,
Mud, water like dirty glass, expressing silence

Of a sort, silence of a rat come out to see,
The great pond and its waste of the lilies, all this

> Had to be imagined as an inevitable knowledge,
> Required, as a necessity requires. (CP, 502)

For all the submission to the external that we see in these two poems, the consolations of the imagination are no less persuasive in "Final Soliloquy of the Interior Paramour."

> Light the first light of evening, as in a room
> In which we rest, and, for small reason, think
> The world imagined is the ultimate good.
>
> This is, therefore, the intensest rendezvous.
> It is in that thought that we collect ourselves,
> Out of all the indifferences, into one thing:
> . . .
> Here, now, we forget each other and ourselves.
> We feel the obscurity of an order, a whole,
> A knowledge, that which arranged the rendezvous.
>
> Within its vital boundary, in the mind
> We say God and the imagination are one . . .
> How high that highest candle lights the dark.
>
> Out of this same light, out of the central mind,
> We make a dwelling in the evening air,
> In which being there together is enough. (CP, 524)

Neither this possibility, nor the possibility explored in the previous two poems, are perfect solutions of the predicament. They are not competing theories but complementary aspects of the same problem. Stevens' remarks on illusion to Hi Simons are relevant here.

> Poetry as a narcotic is escapism in the pejorative sense. But there is a benign escapism in every illusion. The use of the word illusion suggests the simplest way to define the difference between escapism in a pejorative sense and in a non-pejorative sense . . . of course, I

believe in benign illusion. To my way of thinking, the idea of God is an instance of a benign illusion. (*L*, 402)

Even the bareness of "The Plain Sense of Things," that poem hints, may be a benign illusion, since it takes a willed act of imagination to envision it. Stevens knows himself and his predicament well enough to understand that belief is ultimately not the real issue. Without believing or denying either of the possible imaginative extremes, he can inhabit both as benign illusion, as poetic fiction. In a letter to Henry Church, he describes a curious conversation on the subject:

> One evening, a week or so ago, a student at Trinity College came to the office and walked home with me. We talked about this book. I said that I thought that we had reached a point at which we could no longer really believe anything unless we recognized that it was a fiction. The student said that that was an impossibility, that there was no such thing as believing in something that one knew was not true. It is obvious, however, that we are doing that all the time. There are things with respect to which we willingly suspend disbelief; if there is instinctive in us a will to believe, or if there is a will to believe, whether or not it is instinctive, it seems to me that we can suspend disbelief with reference to a fiction as easily as we can suspend it with reference to anything else. There are fictions that are extensions of reality. There are plenty of people who believe in Heaven as definitely as your New England ancestors and my Dutch ancestors believed in it. But Heaven is an extension of reality. (*L*, 430)

Stevens had known the reason for this for a long time.

It is a state, this spring among the politicians
Playing cards. In a village of the indigenes,
One would have still to discover. Among the dogs and dung,
One would continue to contend with one's ideas. (*CP*, 197)

In the same letter to Henry Church quoted above, Stevens says "Of course, in the long run, poetry would be the supreme fiction;

the essence of poetry is change and the essence of change is that it must give pleasure" (L, 430). This is the sort of remark that gladdens the hearts of post-structuralist critics. It is also one of those definitive statements that one has to watch out for, whose meaning needs to be drawn from the context in which it was made. From the remarks in the letter that precede the story about the student from Trinity College, it is clear that Stevens is speaking poetically and not oracularly. Anticipating the critical reception to Notes, Stevens wrote, ". . . I think I am right in saying that in not a single review of Parts of a World was there so much as a suggestion that the book gave the man who read it any pleasure. Now, to give pleasure to an intelligent man, by this sort of thing, is as much as one can expect. . . ." He then goes on as follows:

> It is only when you try to systematize the poems in the NOTES that you conclude that it is not the statement of a philosophic theory. A philosopher is never at rest unless he is systematizing: constructing a theory. But these are Notes; the nucleus of the matter is contained in the title. It is implicit in the title that there can be such a thing as a supreme fiction. (L, 430)

He then describes the conversation with the student from Trinity College and it's in the next paragraph—about the form of the supreme fiction—that he says "the NOTES start out with the idea that it would not take any form: that it would be abstract . . ." and he arrives at the statement about the essence of poetry. Other supreme fictions might not necessarily be abstract: a belief, in, say, a future workers' paradise reached by means of a long struggle in which other social classes are displaced is an instance of a supreme fiction that has been believed and which has worked to realize itself in the actual world. The "abstractness" of the supreme fiction (whose other distinguishing feature is that nobody would have to believe in it) is that the transformations it would effect would all take place in the life of the imagination: the imagination would be its field of play. "The essence of poetry is change" (*L*, 430) for Stevens because the creative mind does not adopt a philosophical program and just stick to it—as Crispin found, poetry was continuous activity. The supreme pleasure only works for as long as it gives a kind of pleasure that is the answer to the imagination's need for change. The change, as it was for Crispin, is the continuous movement from worn out habits of vision to whatever quickens the appetite for reality. Like *The Comedian as the Letter C*, *Notes toward a Supreme Fiction* is, within the context of that continuous activity, just one arrangement of the possibilities. Further on in the letter, Stevens writes: "The truth is that [*Notes*] ought to be one of only a number of books and that, if I had nothing else in the world to do except to sit on a fence and think about things, it would in fact be one of a number of books" (*L*, 431).

The supreme fiction is one part of a whole general process of activity. Poetry is the activity. Not a doctrine, or even a theory. The supreme fiction, as Stevens could have known years before, was another "idea for the purpose of poetry."

> . . . . It may be that every man introduces his own order into the life about him and that the idea of order in general is simply what Bishop Berkeley might have called a fortuitous concourse of personal orders. But still there is order. This is the sort of development you are looking for. But then, I never thought that it was a fixed philosophical proposition that life was a mass of irrelevancies any more than I now know that it is a fixed proposition that every man introduces his own order as part of a general order. These are tentative ideas for the purpose of poetry. (*L*, 293)

That purpose could be described as the seeking of some peculiar kind of happiness: a quickening of consciousness and energy, a feeling of being let into secrets of existence. Stevens described to Hi Simons how he constructed "Anecdote of Canna":

> This occurred to me one late summer afternoon while I was killing time in Washington. The beds of the terraces around the Capitol were filled with canna. The place became a place in which the

President (the "mighty man") was the man walking round and everything became huge, mighty, etc. X is the President. My state of mind became his state of mind. . . . (L, 464)

This account was written in 1944, and by then Stevens had had many occasions to say that "explanations spoil things." But this explanation, it seems to me, actually enhances the poem. It suggests that Stevens' motive for writing the poem was not a desire to write a theory of poetry but pleasure in the step-by-step thinking that he could still remember twenty-five years later.

He speaks in the same letter of the "exhilaration" of reality. Wordsworth experienced it too. The poet in *Resolution and Independence* has an unexpected encounter with the old leech-gatherer, which drives all his ideas out of his consciousness and surprises him into the realization that existence is joy. (The hare already knows it.)

> All things that love the sun are out of doors;
> The sky rejoices in the morning's birth;
> The grass is bright with rain-drops; on the moors
> The hare is running races in her mirth;
> And with her feet she from the plashy earth
> Raises a mist; that, glittering in the sun,
> Runs with her all the way, wherever she doth run.
> (Wordsworth, 284)

J.V. Cunningham movingly describes Stevens' situation with respect to this kind of experience:

> It is a fortuitous experience; it cannot be willed into being, or contrived at need. It is a transitory experience; it cannot be stayed in its going or found when it is gone. Yet though fortuitous and transitory, it has in its moment of being all the persuasion of permanence; it seems—and perhaps in its way it is—a fulfillment of the Absolute. . . .
> Stevens attempted to will it into being. (Cunningham, 241)

Long, long after Crispin abandoned his localism, Stevens met the young Cuban José Rodríguez-Feo. The young poet had begun a correspondence with Stevens over the latter's poetry and they became friends of sorts. Friendships often contain a certain amount of confusion between what people expect of friends and what is actually there. Rodríguez-Feo is writing to a Great Mind. Stevens is like a man on a beach who has been floating bottles out to sea with cryptic messages in them, who finally gets a reply from a country and an individual he had only hopefully imagined. Someone to share the fun, a pleasure-companion. Here are some samples of Stevens' writing in his letters. In 1948–49 Stevens was seventy years old.

> When I go into a fruit store nowadays and find there nothing but the fruits du jour: apples, pears, oranges, I feel like throwing them at the Greek. I expect, and you expect, sapodillas and South Shore bananas and pineapples a foot high with spines fit to stick in the helmet of a wild chieftain.
>
> You probably asked me a lot of questions in your last letter. I ignore them. Why should I answer questions from young philosophers when I receive perfumed notes from Paris? What I really like to have from you is not your tears on the death of Bernanos, say, but news about chickens raised on red peppers and homesick rhapsodies of the Sienese look of far away Havana and news about people I don't know, who are more fascinating to me than all the characters in all the novels of Spain, which I am unable to read. (*L*, 621)
>
> When I have been busy at the office, suddenly I feel that, important as all that is, I am after all losing time and then I read, and again, suddenly, I feel that reading is not enough and that it is time I collected myself and did a poem or two. Thus the need for variety of experience asserts itself and the pressure of obscure cravings makes itself felt even here in Hartford, which is presumably an insensitive mass of insensitive people not to be thought of with Princeton . . . or Havana where poets are like vines that bring color to the structure of the place out of the soil of Cuba or that country menage over which the Señora Consuelo presides with her

malevolent shadow and influence. Even as she plots the purloining of Linda and meditates the suffocation of roosters she is confronted by the sounds and shouts of people from Vigo whom she is afraid even to abduct and imprison in her cellar, say, because there are so many of them and they are too jolly and too full of Malaga wine and cheese and, I hope, sausages. (*L*, 623)

    I realize that a spirit like yours, panting for the company of the erudite and the wise, finds an overwhelming attraction in merely being in places like Princeton and Cambridge, etc., which are so lousy with the erudite and the wise. Providence has, as I say, probably invented colitis so that you could sit on the front porch and respond to Cuba and make something of it, and help to invent or perfect the idea of Cuba in which everyone can have a being just as everyone has a special being in a great church—in the presence of any great object. Your job is to create the spirit of Cuba. (*L*, 654)

What he appreciated from Rodríguez-Feo (and what Rodríguez-Feo did not himself appreciate) was those glimpses of an exotic, chaotic reality—one that set his imagination in motion among delightful characters and objects and scenes. The scenes Rodriguez-Feo describes are like something Stevens himself might have wished he had imagined. In advising the young poet to "create the spirit of Cuba" he again, in spite of all he knew, thought that the spirit of Cuba could be created and not found.

    In the end, he acknowledged that the Absolute could not be willed into existence: he adjusted to the conditions "Of Mere Being" (*OP*, 117). He found a clear-eyed trust in the universe, an intelligent self-forgiveness, and faith, for which he devised a beautiful, poetic emblem.

    The palm at the end of the mind,
    Beyond the last thought, rises
    In the bronze distance,

A gold-feathered bird
Sings in the palm, without human meaning,
Without human feeling, a foreign song.

You know then that it is not the reason
That makes us happy or unhappy.
The bird sings. Its feathers shine.

The palm stands on the edge of space.
The wind moves slowly in the branches.
The bird's fire-fangled feathers dangle down. (OP,
117–118)

But of course, he had known this before too.

Notes

1. Popper describes Hegel's strategy as:
An attempt to evade Kant's refutation of what Kant called "dogmatism" in meta-physics. This refutation is considered by Hegel to hold only for systems which are metaphysical in his more narrow sense, but not for dialectical rationalism, which takes account of the development of reason and is therefore not afraid of contradic-tions. In evading Kant's criticism in this way, Hegel embarks on an extremely dangerous venture which must lead to disaster, for he argues something like this: "Kant refuted rationalism by saying that it must lead to contradictions. I admit that. But it is clear that this argument draws its force from the law of contradiction: it refutes only such systems as accept this law, i.e. such as try to be free from contradictions. It is not dangerous for a system like mine which is prepared to put up with contradictions—that is, for a dialectic system." It is clear that this argument establishes a dogmatism of an extremely dangerous kind—a dogmatism which need no longer be afraid of any sort of attack. For any attack, any criticism of any theory whatsoever, must be based on the method of pointing out some sort of contradic-tion, either within the theory itself or between the theory and some facts. (Popper, 327)

2. It may even predate Hegel.

3. For example: Stevens probably knew the difference between a negress and a bear in heat, a difference which, like the syntax of "The Virgin Carrying a Lantern," seems to have escaped Helen Vendler. This may be one of the fastest misreadings in the history of reading, since it starts with the very first line and never rights itself.

> There are no bears among the roses,
> Only a negress who supposes
> Things false and wrong
>
> About the lantern of the beauty. . . . (CP, 71)

Vendler writes: "If the negress supposes bears, it is because she is acquainted with bears, while the virgin knows only roses . . . The poem may be seen as a rewriting of Blake's lamb and tiger: the virgin is what Melville would have called a radiant ninny, but there is none of Blake's admiration for his tiger embodied in Stevens' figure for the dark, for the heated, and for the bestial in himself" (Vendler, 1984, 18–19). But why should negresses be acquainted with bears? There aren't any bears in the jungle. Maybe because negresses are bestial?

Chapter Two

1. Of which the best is J.V. Cunningham's "Tradition and Modernity: Wallace Stevens," in *Tradition and Poetic Structure* (Denver: Swallow, 1960).
2. Of this stanza, Yvor Winters wrote: "The poet considers an hypothetical paradise, and since he can imagine it only in terms of a projection of the good life as the hedonist understands the good life, he deduces that paradise would become tedious and insipid. . . ." (Winters, 432) But Stevens is only attacking an idea; the paradise that would become tedious and insipid is the paradise that we have imagined. Winters may have imagined a more interesting one, but nobody knows anything about the real paradise, if there is one.
3. I don't choose to dwell here on other theories of influence, such as those of Roy Harvey Pearce, Harold Bloom, and others. I gave some of the objections to these types of "theories" in chapter 1. For a thorough critique of Bloom's theory, see B.J. Leggett's *Wallace Stevens and Poetic Theory* (Chapel Hill: University of North Carolina Press, 1987): 42 ff.

Chapter Three

1. "Man", of course, is Stevens' character. I use the term here when I am following the track of Stevens' thinking, for a couple of reasons. First, I don't want to create a confusion of terms: second, I think that when I am working inside of Stevens' ideas as they are formally expressed in poems, it is important, as far as possible, not to substitute my own language and ideas for his own. When I speak for myself, I shall continue to avoid these unsatisfactory usages.
2. See above, chapter 2, and *Souvenirs and Prophecies*, 38.
3. Helen Vendler, in a note to *Words Chosen Out of Desire* (1985, 80), describes poetry as "the projection of fact (e.g. a failed romantic endeavour) onto the plane of language . . ." and declares that "there is no lyric poet who does not have the aim of 'self-expression', from Sappho to Ashberry" (Vendler, 1985, 6). She is justifying her contention that *Le Monocle de Mon Oncle* is really about the failure of Stevens' marriage. The metaphor she uses to describe what poetry is is an unintelligible and unexamined commonplace that has passed from psychology into universal circulation; nevertheless it is easy enough to recognize in this definition the simplest romantic subjectivism. Vendler has defined *all* lyric poetry as essentially taking the form of Keats' sonnet "On

reading Chapman's Homer": a person (real or invented) has something happen to them and then they say how it made them feel.

The ultimate tendency of the romantic-subjective poetry which has to be "fantastic and wonderful" to be interesting, is towards Poe's *Philosophy of Composition* (see chapter 1 above), a theory that does not contain the terms for talking about problems, solutions, or moving beyond those solutions to new imaginative possibilities. These are facts also, and Vendler herself, discussing the poem "Local Objects" (Vendler, 1984, 6–9), gives the closest thing we will probably ever have to an explanation, from the perspective of Stevens' personal life, of why he wrote about these and not about his failed marriage or his social life.

4. Stevens' criticism of Freud in *Le Monocle de Mon Oncle* applies also to (late) Tolstoy's ideal of renunciation. What if Prince Nekhlyudov or Ivan Ilyich or Pierre Bezukhov, having renounced everything false and wicked, found when they woke up one morning that they had the same restlessness, the same inability to accommodate themselves to their own ideas, even the same old lusts and vanities, behaving as if they were just as compelling as sacrifice seemed last week? Which is what kept happening to Tolstoy.

5. In his essay "American Painting," Paul Rosenfeld describes the epoch that produced Wallace Stevens "the moment of the root-taking of an American culture." Stevens came to artistic maturity when Alfred Stieglitz, William Carlos Williams, Robert McAlmon, and Robert Coady, among others, were proclaiming the need for a true American art that would portray the changes that had occurred since the "root-taking" a generation before. Rooting one's "intelligence" in the "soil," to use the language of Crispin, was the only way to achieve the American art they envisioned. In relation to the dominance of these localists in America, Stevens was like the little magazine *Secession* in its opposition to *The Dial*, *The Little Review*, and *Broom*. *Secession* boldly announced its dream of avoiding immersion in popular literary trends and declared a determination to publish "the unknown pathbreaking artist" and to support stylistic experiment. Just as *Secession's* main driving force was a sure sense of what it did not want to be, Stevens' secession from current fads pushed him beyond the localism of "From the Journal of Crispin" and toward "The Comedian" and a life as a "pathbreaking artist. . . ." (Strom, 134)

6. By the dead reckoning of a Marxist, Socratic ignorance is inconceivable. What Stevens does not know (but seems to suspect), according to Stanley Burnshaw, is that he is rapidly approaching obsolescence. "[As one of the] . . . Acutely conscious members of a class menaced by the clashes between capital and labor, [Stevens is] in the throes of philosophical adjustment. And [his] words have intense value and meaning to the sectors within the class whose confusions [he] articulate[s]." Pangloss doesn't know it but he is a lackey of imperialism. It would not be worth bringing up such strangely dated criticism (Burnshaw himself has different views now) except that there are still critics who sing the same song about Stevens: Fredric Jameson, for instance, who seems to think that Stevens made raids on the tropics (read Third World) and stripped them of poetic ideas:

. . . [Stevens'] is clearly a peculiar view of the Third World, which one might seek to concretize by the experience of the world tour, the liner cruise through the islands, a peculiarly disengaged luxury tourist's contemplative contact with ports and maps (a specific moment, one would think, of aristocratic or moneyed tourism in the 1920s, which has little socially in common with the present day). This impoverished experience reconfirms our notion of the underlying purely epistemo-logical stance of Stevens' work—a detached subject contemplating a static object in a suspension of praxis or even rootedness—and is documented in Stevens' one autobiographical "novel" or narrative, "The Comedian as the Letter C." Yet if this is the phenomenological experience, the "social equivalent" of Stevens' fascination with place-names, it also betrays a far deeper social and economic source which is that of the consumption of luxury products and objects at a particular moment in the development of Western capitalism, and reflects, one might say, a kind of luxury-mercantilist *Weltanschaung*, as so many sources for imported goods. . . . (Jameson, 184)

An awesome transition from speculation to accusation, so intellectually daring, so *rigorous* in that we don't even need to know whether Jameson is talking about a cruise that Stevens actually took, or one that he only thought about taking. What's the difference? All those people who took cruises, who might have only daydreamed about "concretizing their views of the Third World" by taking a cruise. Oh, the wickedness of it.

Chapter Four

1. This letter, dated 8 June 1916, is in the Huntington Library's collection of the papers of Wallace Stevens. It is reproduced here with the Library's permission. Williams' typescript of the poem, with the suggested changes, is in the same folder.
2. See above, chapter 3.

Chapter Five

1. *The Rime* does not always maintain the dignity it is supposed to, being padded here and there with unidiomatic metrical filler as in "Water, water everywhere, / And all the boards did shrink."
2. I must clarify something: When I say that all the phenomena of the physical world can be explained by the theory, we don't really know that. Most phenomena we are familiar with involve such *tremendous* numbers of electrons that it's hard for our poor minds to follow that complexity. In such situations, we can use the theory to figure roughly what ought to happen and that *is* what happens, roughly, in those circumstances. But if we arrange in the laboratory an experiment involving just a *few* electrons in *simple* circumstances, then we can calculate what might happen very accurately, and we can measure it very accurately, too. Whenever we do such experiments, the theory of quantum electrodynamics works very well.

We physicists are always checking to see if there is something the matter with the theory. That's the game, because if there *is* something the matter, it's interesting! But so far, we have found nothing wrong with the theory of quantum electrodynamics. It is, therefore, I would say, the jewel of physics— our proudest possession. (Feynman, 8)

   3. Faced with the necessity of survival, for making order, in a teeming and chaotic world—"a booming, buzzing chaos," as William James called it—the brain is highly plastic and adapts itself at each moment. The infant, the human infant at least, is born into chaos, at least so far as complex perceptions and cognitions go. The infant immediately starts exploring the world, looking, feeling, touching, smelling, as all higher animals do, from the moment of birth. Sensation alone is not enough; it must be combined with movement, with action. Movement and sensation together become integrated to form a "category," a coherent brain response, a category which is the antecedent of a "meaning." Subsequent explorations—feeling the same object at different times, in different contexts—are never quite the same, so that the initial category is revised, recategorized, and re-recategorized, again and again. Given this incessant recategorization, no perception, no image, no memory, one would expect, would ever be precisely repeated or the same. Yet through this structuring and restructuring, the infant, the growing individual, constructs a self and a world. (Sacks, 48)

   4. *The One of Fictive Music* is explained by Stevens as "all the things that live in memory and imagination" (*L*, 297).

Works Cited

Abrams, M. H. *Natural Supernaturalism*. New York: W.W. Norton & Co., 1971.

Aiken, Conrad. "The Ivory Tower" *The New Republic* 19 (1919):58–60.

Axelrod, Steven Gould, and Helen Deese. *Critical Essays on Wallace Stevens*. Boston: G.K. Hall, 1988.

Bates, Milton J. *Wallace Stevens: A Mythology of Self*. Berkeley: University of California Press, 1985.

Bloom, Harold. *The Poems of Our Climate*. Ithaca: Cornell University Press, 1977.

Burnshaw, Stanley. "Turmoil in the Middle Ground" (1935). In *Critical Essays on Wallace Stevens*. Edited by Steven Gould Axelrod and Helen Deese. Boston: G.K. Hall, 1988.

Carroll, Joseph. *Wallace Stevens' Supreme Fiction: A New Romanticism*. Baton Rouge: Louisiana State University Press, 1987.

Connolly, Cyril. *Enemies of Promise*. London: Penguin Books, 1961.

Cunningham, J.V. "Tradition and Modernity: Wallace Stevens." In *The Collected Essays of J.V. Cunningham*. Denver: Swallow, 1976.

Feynman, Richard. *QED*. Princeton: Princeton University Press, 1985.

Jameson, Fredric. "Wallace Stevens." In *Critical Essays on Wallace Stevens*. Edited by Steven Gould Axelrod and Helen Deese. Boston: G.K. Hall, 1988.

Keats, John. "On First Looking into Chapman's Homer." In *English Romantic Writers*. Edited by David Perkins. New York: Harcourt Brace Jovanovich, 1967.

Kermode, Frank. *Wallace Stevens*. London: Oliver and Boyd, 1960.

Leggett, B. J. *Wallace Stevens and Poetic Theory*. Chapel Hill: University of North Carolina Press, 1987.

Litz, A. Walton. *Introspective Voyager*. New York: Oxford University Press, 1972.

Miller, J. Hillis. "Wallace Stevens' Poetry of Being." In *The Act of the Mind: Essays on the Poetry of Wallace Stevens*. Edited by Roy Harvey Pearce and J. Hillis Miller. Baltimore: Johns Hopkins University Press, 1965.

———. *Poets of Reality*. The Belknap Press. Cambridge: Harvard University Press, 1965.

———. *The Linguistic Moment*. Princeton: Princeton University Press, 1985.

Mills, Ralph Jr. "Wallace Stevens: The Image of the Rock." In *Wallace Stevens: A Collection of Critical Essays*. Edited by Marie Borroff. Englewood Cliffs, NJ: Prentice-Hall, 1963.

Pater, Walter. *Appreciations*. London: Macmillan, 1889.

Pearce, Roy Harvey. *The Continuity of American Poetry*. Princeton: Princeton University Press, 1961.

———. "Wallace Stevens: The Last Lesson of the Master." In *The Act of the Mind: Essays on the Poetry of Wallace Stevens*. Baltimore: Johns Hopkins University Press, 1965.

Perloff, Marjorie. "Pound / Stevens: Whose Era?" In *New Literary History: A Journal of Theory and Interpretation* 13 (1982):485–510.

———."The Supreme Fiction and the Impasse of Modernist Lyric." In *Wallace Stevens: The Poetics of Modernism*. Edited by Albert Gelpi. New York: Cambridge University Press, 1985.

Poe, Edgar Allan. "The Philosophy of Composition" (1846). In *Edgar Allan Poe: Essays and Reviews*. New York: Library of America, 1984.

Popper, Karl R. *Conjectures and Refutations: The Growth of Scientific Knowledge*. New York: Harper & Row, 1968.

Richardson, Joan. *Wallace Stevens: The Early Years, 1879–1923*. New York: Beech Tree Books, 1986.

Sacks, Oliver. "Neurology and the Soul." *The New York Review of Books* 37 (November 22, 1990): 44–50.

Sidney, Sir Philip. *Sir Philip Sidney*. The Oxford Authors. Oxford: Oxford University Press, 1990.

Stevens, Holly. "Bits of Remembered Time." *Southern Review* 7 (1971): 651–657.

Stevens, Wallace. *The Collected Poems of Wallace Stevens*. New York: Knopf, 1954; Vintage Books, 1982.

————. *Letters of Wallace Stevens*. Edited by Holly Stevens. New York: Knopf, 1966.

————. *Opus Posthumous*. New York: Knopf, 1957; Vintage Books, 1982.

————. *The Palm at the End of the Mind*. New York: Knopf, 1971. Reprint. Hamden: Archon Books, 1984.

————. *Souvenirs and Prophecies: The Young Wallace Stevens*. Edited by Holly Stevens. New York: Knopf, 1977.

Strom, Martha. "Wallace Stevens' Revisions of Crispin's Journal: a Reaction Against the 'Local'." In *Critical Essays on Wallace Stevens*. Edited by Steven Gould Axelrod and Helen Deese. Boston: G.K. Hall, 1988.

Untermeyer, Louis. "The Ivory Tower—II." *The New Republic* 19 (1919): 60–61.

Vendler, Helen. *On Extended Wings: Wallace Stevens' Longer Poems*. Cambridge: Harvard University Press, 1969.

————. *Wallace Stevens: Words Chosen Out of Desire*. Knoxville: University of Tennessee Press, 1984.

Voltaire. *Candide* (1759). In *The Portable Voltaire*. Edited by Ben Ray Rodman. New York: Penguin Books, 1977.

Williams, William Carlos. Letter to Wallace Stevens, 8 June 1916. WAS 12. Wallace Stevens Papers. Huntington Library, San Marino, California.

Wilson, Edmund. *Letters on Literature and Politics, 1912–1972*. Edited by Elena Wilson. New York: Farrar Straus and Giroux, 1977.

Winters, Yvor. *In Defense of Reason* (1943). Reprint. Athens, Ohio: Swallow, 1987.

Wordsworth, William. "Preface to the Second Edition of the *Lyrical Ballads*". In *English Romantic Writers*. Edited by David Perkins. New York: Harcourt Brace Jovanovich, 1967.

Index

Poems and other works cited are listed under their respective authors.

149